THE
BIBLE IS A
CATHOLIC
BOOK

JIMMY AKIN

Published by Catholic Answers, Inc.

2020 Gillespie Way

El Cajon, California 92020

1-888-291-8000 orders

619-387-0042 fax

catholic.com

Printed in the United States of America

Cover and interior design by Russell Graphic Design

978-1-68357-141-4

978-1-68357-142-1 Kindle

978-1-68357-143-8 ePub

To the memory of my grandmother,
Rosalie Octava Beard Burns,
who gave me my first Bible.

CONTENTS

The Bible, the Word of God, and You

The Bible can be intimidating. It's a big, thick book—much longer than most books people read. It's also ancient. The most recent part of it was penned almost 2,000 years ago. That means it's not written in a modern style. It can seem strange and unfamiliar to a contemporary person. Even more intimidating is that it shows us our sins and makes demands on our lives.

No wonder some people hesitate to take the plunge and start reading the Bible!

But each of the things that can make it intimidating is actually a benefit:

- Because the Bible is so large, it contains a *great deal* of valuable information. If it were short, it wouldn't tell us nearly as much.

- The fact that it was written so long ago testifies to its timeless message. Its teachings aren't tied to just one time or culture. They have endured, and by reading Scripture we experience the joy of discovering the story of God's dealings with mankind.

- Finally, it's important that it reveals our sins to us. We need wake-up calls that shake us out of our feeble attempts to rationalize what we're doing wrong. And Scripture is quick to assure us of God's love for us. "For God so loved the world that he gave his only Son, that whoever believes in him should not perish but have eternal life" (John 3:16).

The Bible is an inestimable gift from God. It's his word in written form—something each of us should cherish and study regularly.

Some groups of Christians try to claim the Bible for themselves. They make it sound like the Catholic Church is opposed to Scripture. Some even claim that the Church "hates" the Bible.

But as we'll see, all Christians owe an enormous debt to the Catholic Church, for it was through the Church that the Bible was given to the world. Jesus himself founded the Catholic Church. He appointed its first leaders, and they were the ones who—under the inspiration of the Holy Spirit—wrote the books of the New Testament, which completed and became the capstone of all the scriptures that had come before.

The Holy Spirit then guided the Catholic Church to discern which books belonged in the Bible and which did not. This involved the crucial process of sorting the true scriptures from all of the false ones that existed.

The Catholic Church laboriously copied the scriptures in the age before the printing press, when every book—including lengthy ones like the Bible—had to be written by hand. It thus preserved these books through the centuries, unlike so many ancient works that have now been lost.

The Catholic Church is why we have the Bible today, and everyone should be grateful for the gift that, by the grace of God, it has given to the world.

The Bible is a Catholic book!

1

The Word of God
Before the Bible

IN THE BEGINNING WAS THE WORD

How the world began is a question people everywhere ask.
It's a human universal.

Pagan cultures thought the world was made by their
gods and goddesses. Some myths claimed that the gods
reproduced sexually to make the elements of the world.
Others held that there was a fierce battle among the gods,
and the world was formed from the corpses of the losers.
Mankind was then created as a slave race to relieve the gods
of drudgery.

The book of Genesis set the record straight: The world
was not produced by a multitude of finite gods. It was the
creation of a single, great God—one supreme and supremely
good Being who is behind everything.

Because of his infinite, unlimited power, he didn't need
to use anything to make the world, as the pagans thought.
He didn't need to mate with a goddess. He didn't need to
battle other gods and make the world from their corpses.

He simply *spoke*, and the elements of the world sprang into existence: "God said, 'Let there be light'; and there was light" (Gen. 1:3).

God made a good world, and to crown his creation, he made man—not to relieve him of drudgery but to serve as his representative, ruling over creation:

> God created man in his own image, in the image of God he created him; male and female he created them. And God blessed them, and God said to them, "Be fruitful and multiply, and fill the earth and subdue it; and have dominion over the fish of the sea and over the birds of the air and over every living thing that moves upon the earth." And God saw everything that he had made, and behold, it was very good (Gen. 1:27–28, 31).

Through the ages, God continued to speak. Even when man fell into sin, he sent the prophets to correct him and call him back to communion with his Creator. Eventually, he sent his Son, Jesus, to redeem mankind and to proclaim his definitive word to us:

> In many and various ways God spoke of old to our Fathers by the prophets; but in these Last Days he has spoken to us by a Son, whom he appointed the heir of all things, through whom also he created the world (Heb. 1:1–2).

The Gospel of John reveals more about God's Son and how the world was made:

> In the beginning was the Word, and the Word was with God, and the Word was God. He was in the beginning

with God; all things were made through him, and without him was not anything made that was made (John 1:1–3).

This reveals that Jesus—God's Son—was the Word he spoke when he created the world and everything in it. When God said, "Let there be light," it was through Jesus that this happened.

Because Jesus was there in the beginning—one of the uncreated, divine Persons of the Trinity—he is the original and supreme Word of God. All of God's other words are shadows of him.

This is important to remember, because some today use the phrase "word of God" as if it just meant "the Bible." Although the Bible is important, the word of God is not confined to or only found in it. First and foremost, Jesus Christ himself is the Word of God, and there are other expressions of it, only some of which are found in Scripture.

THE SPIRIT OF GOD

The Father and the Son are two of the divine Persons of the Holy Trinity, but what about the third—the Holy Spirit?

Theologians tell us that every time God performs an action in the world, all three Persons play a role. For example, to save mankind, God the Father sent the Son to redeem us, and he and the Son together send the Holy Spirit to draw us back to him and bring his grace into our lives. Consequently, it's no surprise that we find the Spirit of God also took part in the creation of the world:

In the beginning God created the heavens and the earth. The earth was without form and void, and darkness was upon the face of the deep; and the Spirit of God was moving over the face of the waters (Gen. 1:1–2).

In the biblical languages, the word for *spirit* is the same as the word for *breath*, so Scripture indicates that God created by both his word and his spirit, or breath:

By the word of the Lord the heavens were made, and all their host by the breath of his mouth (Ps. 33:6).

Although the doctrine of the Trinity would not be fully revealed until the New Testament age, this passage shows how both the Son (the Word) and the Spirit were active in creation. The image the passage uses is based on the fact that, when we speak, it is our breath that carries our words. In speech, our breath and our words are intertwined. They always go together, and so it is with God. When God sent prophets, it was the Holy Spirit who gave them God's word. The prophet Zechariah records how God's people refused to listen to the message that the Holy Spirit gave through the prophets:

They made their hearts like adamant lest they should hear the law and the words which the Lord of hosts had sent by his Spirit through the former prophets. Therefore, great wrath came from the Lord of hosts (Zech. 7:12).

The Holy Spirit continued to be active in the New Testament era, even after Jesus' ministry. At the Last Supper, Jesus told his disciples:

I have yet many things to say to you, but you cannot bear them now. When the Spirit of truth comes, he will guide you into all the truth; for he will not speak on his own authority, but whatever he hears he will speak, and he will declare to you the things that are to come. He will glorify me, for he will take what is mine and declare it to you (John 16:12–14).

One of the ways the Holy Spirit communicates God's word to us is in writing. The Latin word for *writing* is *scriptura*, and so the writings that the Holy Spirit produced are known as *Scripture*. St. Peter says:

First of all, you must understand this, that no prophecy of Scripture is a matter of one's own interpretation, because no prophecy ever came by the impulse of man, but men moved by the Holy Spirit spoke from God (2 Pet. 1:20–21).

St. Peter indicates that, although the human author was responsible on one level for writing a book of Scripture, on a more fundamental level it was the Holy Spirit working through them. The name for the process by which the Holy Spirit did this is *inspiration*. This word comes from Latin roots that mean "to breathe into" (*in* + *spirare*).

To say that a book of Scripture is inspired is to say that God has breathed the words it contains. This is the way the New Testament describes inspiration in Greek: it is God- (*theos*) breathed (*pneustos*). Thus St. Paul says:

All Scripture is inspired by God [*theopneustos*] and profitable for teaching, for reproof, for correction, and for training in righteousness, that the man of God may be complete, equipped for every good work (2 Tim. 3:16–17).

To say that Scripture is inspired or God-breathed does not mean that the biblical authors were mere secretaries, writing down what they heard God dictate by an inner voice. The Holy Spirit worked through them in an organic way, using their minds, talents, and life experiences. When St. Paul says, "I myself am an Israelite, a descendant of Abraham, a member of the tribe of Benjamin" (Rom. 11:1), he is speaking of himself as a human being, and he is serving as a true author. The Second Vatican Council explained the process of inspiration this way:

> To compose the sacred books, God chose certain men who, all the while he employed them in this task, made full use of their powers and faculties so that, though he acted in them and by them, it was as true authors that they consigned to writing whatever he wanted written, and no more (*Dei Verbum* 11).

Today, we are fortunate to have Scripture, an inspired collection of writings that convey God's word to us. However, it's important to remember that this has not always been the case. In fact, for most of human history, God's people *didn't* have Scripture.

THE AGE OF THE SPOKEN WORD

Speech is a human universal, but writing is not. There was an age before writing had been invented.

Although we don't know the exact date that writing began, we do have a pretty good idea of how it developed because archaeologists have discovered a trove of ancient drawings, artifacts, and inscriptions that reveal its history.

The earliest human signs were a kind of protowriting that consisted of pictures and markings that carried only a basic meaning. We often can't tell what that meaning was, but sometimes we can. For example, we have cave paintings that clearly represent horses, stars, people, and spears. We also have artifacts with notches or knots that were used to count items.

Recreation of a cave painting from the Ardéche valley in France, 35,000–30,000 B.C.

The signs used in protowriting convey only a limited amount of information. They can't represent everything that we can communicate in speech. For this reason, speech was the primary means humans had to communicate with each other. It was the age of the spoken word—the first phase of human history.

God made himself known to man in this period. Genesis shows God giving the commission to have dominion over the earth and to rule and care for it on his behalf. It records him settling Adam in the garden of Eden, giving him the commandment regarding what he could eat, allowing him to name the animals, and being both just and merciful with him when he fell into sin. The *Catechism of the Catholic Church* (CCC) explains:

> God, who creates and conserves all things by his word, provides men with constant evidence of himself in created realities. And furthermore, wishing to open up the way to heavenly salvation, he manifested himself to

our first parents from the beginning. He invited them to intimate communion with himself and clothed them with resplendent grace and justice.

This revelation was not broken off by our first parents' sin. After the fall, God buoyed them up with the hope of salvation, by promising redemption; and he has never ceased to show his solicitude for the human race. For he wishes to give eternal life to all those who seek salvation by patience in well-doing (54–55).

All this took place at the dawn of human history. God thus came to man and made his word known even before the development of writing.

THE AGE OF THE WRITTEN WORD

The archaeological record reveals when writing began. It didn't happen everywhere all at once, and forms of proto-writing continued to be used in many places. But in two locations—Mesopotamia and Egypt—the first systems of true writing appeared.

Around 3300 B.C., the Mesopotamians began to write on clay tablets using pictograms, or picture writing, and over the next few centuries these became progressively more sophisticated. By around 2600 B.C., they had developed into cuneiform, a system of wedge-shaped marks pressed into clay. These included symbols that represented the syllables of their languages, so anything you could say out loud you could now preserve in writing.

By 3100 B.C., the Egyptians had begun developing their own writing system, which eventually resulted in the hieroglyphs for which Egypt is famous. Before these were deciphered in the nineteenth century, it was thought they were pictograms, but it turned out they were a sophisticated system that incorporated an alphabet, so anything you could say could be written down in full.

Writing didn't catch on everywhere. It took centuries for that to happen, and different peoples adopted it at widely different times. The earliest Chinese writing didn't begin until around 1300 B.C., the Mayans began to write around 300 B.C., and the Cherokee tribe in North America didn't have writing until 200 years ago!

Hieroglyphs (above) & Cuneiform (below)

What about the Hebrews? The earliest alphabet used by the Hebrews is known as the *Proto-Sinaitic script*. It is used in inscriptions found in the Sinai Peninsula, between Egypt and Israel. These inscriptions date to around 1600 B.C. Although scholars agree that this script was used to write a language that belonged to the same family as Hebrew, it isn't clear that Hebrew itself was being spoken at the time. Languages develop over centuries through a long, slow process, and we don't have clear evidence that Hebrew was being spoken until about 1000 B.C.

Just because writing existed didn't mean everyone understood it. Very few people at that time were capable of reading—often only government officials and priests could read. In fact, hieroglyphs have the name they do because they were used by the Egyptian priests, and so they counted as sacred (Greek, *hieros*) carvings (*gluphai*). Even those who could read usually didn't write. That was a task performed by professional scribes. If a king or a priest—or anyone else—wanted something written down, he would have a scribe do it for him.

Proto-Sinaitic inscription

Though writing had been invented, most people were still, effectively, living in the age of the spoken word. The early events of Genesis all took place before writing was invented, and even though it was in use by the time of Abraham, he and the other patriarchs were operating in an almost exclusively oral environment.

In the Bible, the first mention of anyone writing something down doesn't occur until after the Exodus was underway. When God wanted a particular event remembered, he said, "Write this as a memorial in a book and recite it in the ears of Joshua" (Exod. 17:14). It made sense for the Hebrews to use writing at this time because Moses grew up among people who could write. He had been raised in Pharaoh's household (Exod. 2:1–10), and Pharaoh was the ruler and chief priest of Egypt.

But how do we know about the things that preceded the Hebrews' use of writing?

TRADITION!

Any time information is passed from one person to another, it is an example of tradition. The word *tradition* comes from the Latin root *tradere*, which means "to hand over" or "to pass on."

Because our culture is highly literate, we focus on information being passed down in written form—in written tradition—and so we often overlook the way information is passed down in oral cultures, which is by oral tradition.

But that was the way most people got their information in the ancient world, and it worked well. From one generation to another, people would orally pass on the information that was needed—about their history, their land, their skills. The method worked well enough that writing didn't have to be invented for thousands of years, and it's why writing didn't catch on everywhere all at once. Peoples living near literate cultures could go hundreds of years without developing a literature of their own.

One reason oral tradition worked so well is that there were ways of transmitting it in a controlled, accurate fashion. Not just anyone could be a *tradent*—an authorized bearer of tradition. To qualify, a person had to have a good memory, good communication skills, and specialized knowledge of the subject on which he was an authority.

Tradents memorized information by putting it in a memorable form, like when a modern speaker learns the outline of his talk before he gives it in public. Often, ancient tradents would structure information using meter, rhyme, and melody, so that the lore they had to impart took the form of poetry or song. Famous examples include the ancient Greek rhapsodes, who memorized and then performed lengthy works like Homer's *Iliad* and *Odyssey*.

One way of structuring information was what scholars call a *chiasm*. This is a way of ordering information around key words or themes in a kind of inverted structure, like the steps of a pyramid. A simple example of a chiasm is Jesus' saying, "The last will be first, and the first last" (Matt. 20:16). This saying has the following structure:

A: The *last*
　　B: will be *first*
　　B': and the *first*
A': *last*

Chiasms are useful memory tools, because if you can remember the first half of the structure, you know what the second half will be. The example above is short, but ancient authors—including Homer—used longer, more complex ones to organize large amounts of information.

These techniques were used among the Hebrews. The book of Genesis is built around a series of chiasms,[1] and scholars have generally concluded that the oldest portions of the Old Testament are found in certain poems or songs, such as the Blessing of Jacob (Gen. 49), the Song of the Sea (Exod. 15), the Blessing of Moses (Deut. 33), and the Song of Deborah (Judg. 5). These are often held to represent ancient oral traditions that were eventually incorporated into Scripture.

The important thing is that before he began to inspire Scripture, God used and guided the traditions of his people through the long ages before the first biblical author began to write.

THE FIRST BOOKS OF SCRIPTURE WRITTEN

Eventually, God inspired the first biblical author. Precisely who this was is debated.

The books of the Old Testament generally don't say when they were written. Sometimes the authors will date specific things. For example, Isaiah tells us that the vision found in chapter six of his book was something he saw "in the year that King Uzziah died" (i.e., 740 B.C.), but that doesn't tell us when the whole book was issued.

The biblical authors were communicating a timeless message that was meant to last forever, but modern writers have been very curious about the exact times the individual authors wrote.

Because it deals with the creation of the world, the book of Genesis discusses the earliest events, but that doesn't mean it was written first. Genesis belongs to a set of five books, which also includes Exodus, Leviticus, Numbers, and Deuteronomy. Together, they are referred to as the *Pentateuch* (Greek, *pentateukhos*, or "five books"). Because they are written to form a set, scholars have generally held that they, or most of them, were published at about the same time.

Historically, the common view was that Moses wrote them, which would place them either in the 1400s B.C. or the 1200s B.C., depending on when one dates the Exodus. But there are reasons to question this view.

Although Moses is the key figure in these books, and they do record traditions that go back to him, they never claim—as a whole—to be written by him. They also contain an account of his death (Deut. 34), and the final form of these books clearly came after Israel had a monarchy, for Genesis looks back on events "before any king reigned over the Israelites" (Gen. 36:31).

A theory known as the *Documentary Hypothesis* became popular in the nineteenth and twentieth centuries. According to this theory, the Pentateuch is based on four documents (the Yahwist, Elohist, Priestly, and Deuteronomistic sources) that were written between the tenth and sixth centuries B.C. and later combined and published, perhaps around the fifth century B.C. In the last few decades, the Documentary Hypothesis has come under increasing criticism from both conservative and liberal scholars, and at present there is no consensus.

If the books of the Pentateuch weren't the first ones written, which book might have been? Some have pointed to the book of Job, whose central figure appears to live in the age of the patriarchs, before Israel became a nation. But even today we write books about revered figures from the past, so this doesn't tell us when Job was composed.

Some of the early biblical authors were prophets. Figures such as Isaiah, Hosea, Amos, and Micah all wrote in the eighth century B.C.

The Church doesn't have a position on precisely when individual books of Scripture were written or how they were composed. It leaves these matters to scholars. From a perspective of faith, the important thing is that God began to give his inspired word to man. The precise dates on which he did so are secondary.

THE CANON BEGINS TO FORM

Scholars frequently discuss a concept known as the *canon* of Scripture. This is based on the Greek word *kanôn*, which means a rule or measuring rod. It came to mean an authoritative standard, and so the canon of Scripture is the collection of writings that are divinely authoritative.

The Pentateuch was the first authoritative collection of books. These books tell how the people of Israel came to be, as well as God's law for Israel, so they became the core books of Scripture for his people and thus the first part of the biblical canon.

The importance of these books is indicated by their name in Hebrew. They are called the *Torah*—a word meaning "instruction." They contain the fundamental instructions God gave Israel. Later, when the Old Testament was translated into Greek, they became known as *the Law*

(Greek, *nomos*), which is why they're referred to as the Law of Moses.

They became an authoritative collection early. This is shown by the fact that the Samaritans have their own Pentateuch. The Samaritans are descended from the ten northern tribes of Israel. They seceded and formed their own nation around 930 B.C., resulting in the northern kingdom of Israel and the southern kingdom of Judah. They were conquered by the Assyrians around 723 B.C., and many were deported, but there is still a community of Samaritans in Israel. They worship Yahweh, the God of Israel, though they do so on Mt. Gerizim, in their own territory, rather than in Jerusalem.

They have a version of the Torah, known as the *Samaritan Pentateuch*, that includes the same books as the Jewish one and differs only in minor details. This indicates that it has an early date and was considered authoritative—canonical—from early times. It's also significant because the Samaritans accept as canonical *only* the five books of Moses. They don't accept the other books of the Old Testament, which suggests that the Pentateuch was the first group to be canonized and that the canon gradually expanded after this time.

NEW BOOKS OF SCRIPTURE COMPOSED

The ten centuries leading up to the time of Christ were an active period. It was when the Old Testament took shape.

The Pentateuch ends with the death of Moses, and the story of what happened next is continued in a series of historical books. The first, Joshua, tells of the conquest of the promised land. The book of Judges then records how God repeatedly delivered his people from oppression through a series of divinely chosen military leaders. Ruth focuses on the life of a woman who was an ancestor of Israel's most famous king, David.

Israel's history continues in 1 and 2 Samuel, 1 and 2 Kings, and 1 and 2 Chronicles. Each of these was originally a single book, but they are divided in two in modern Bibles. The books of Samuel tell the story of the last of Israel's judges, how the monarchy was established under King Saul, and how it was passed to King David.

The books of Kings cover the final stage of David's life and how Solomon succeeded him. Following Solomon's time, the nation split in two, with the ten northern tribes seceding and forming the kingdom of Israel, leaving the southern tribes as the kingdom of Judah. The story of these two kingdoms is then related, until Israel is conquered and deported by the Assyrian empire around 723 B.C. and Judah is conquered and deported by the Babylonian empire around 587 B.C., beginning the Babylonian Exile.

The books of Chronicles cover the same period as the books of Samuel and Kings, but they focus on the southern kingdom and provide a supplemental theological perspective on the events.

Ezra and Nehemiah, which were originally one book, cover events after the Babylonian Exile. They deal with the people's return to the land of Judah and the rebuilding of the temple.

Esther also deals with the Babylonian Exile, and it is often grouped with the historical books. However, according to Pope St. John Paul II, this book has "the character of allegorical and moral narrative rather than history properly so-called".[2]

God also began to inspire what are known as *wisdom* books. They are devoted to philosophical reflection and the worship of God. The book of Job is a meditation on human suffering, while Ecclesiastes is devoted to the quest for meaning in life. The Song of Solomon celebrates the love of man and woman, and Proverbs offers practical advice for daily living. By far the longest wisdom book is Psalms, which is a collection of hymns.

The final type of book God inspired in the Old Testament period is *prophetic*. Several of these books are significantly longer than the others, so they are known as the *major prophets*. They consist of Isaiah, Jeremiah (together with the short book of Lamentations), Ezekiel, and Daniel. These prophets all relate to the Babylonian Exile in one way or another.

By contrast, the *minor prophets* are generally shorter. There are twelve such books, and they were originally collected in a single volume called *the Twelve*. However, in Christian Bibles they are listed separately. The minor prophets lived between the 800s and 400s B.C., meaning they covered the period both before and after the Babylonian Exile.

THE LAST OLD TESTAMENT BOOKS

The books we've covered so far are considered canonical by all Christians. They are often called *protocanonical* books because they were the first (Greek, *prôtos*) to achieve universal agreement about their status as Scripture. Other books, which took longer to be established, are called *deuterocanonical* books, because agreement on their status came second (Greek, *deuteros*).

In the Protestant community, it is common to hear people say that after Malachi—the last minor prophet—there were "four hundred silent years" in which God inspired no Scripture. However, this is not true. The inspiration of Scripture continued right up until the New Testament.

Two books written in this period are Tobit, which tells the story of God's mercy on a righteous man and his family; and Judith, which describes how God used a righteous woman to deliver his people. Although sometimes grouped with the historical books, according to St. John Paul II, they, like Esther, "have the character of allegorical and moral narrative rather than history properly so-called."[3]

Two books that are historical are 1 and 2 Maccabees. These chronicle how, after the Babylonian Exile, a priestly family known as the Maccabees threw off the yoke of pagan oppression. The basic story is told in 1 Maccabees, and 2 Maccabees provides a supplemental perspective, just as the books of Chronicles do for those of Samuel and Kings.

God also inspired wisdom literature in this period, resulting in the books of Sirach and Wisdom. The first is similar to Proverbs, whereas the second was written to help Jews respond to Greeks ideas. Wisdom is likely the last book of the Old Testament period, being written in the first century B.C. or the early first century A.D.

Baruch is a prophetic work attributed to Jeremiah's secretary of the same name and set during the Babylonian Exile (Bar. 1:1–4). The sixth and final chapter of the book—called the letter of Jeremiah—takes the form of a letter written by the prophet to the exiles in Babylon.

God sometimes inspired books that contained material he had already placed in other books. These could be condensed versions of the original. The most famous is Deuteronomy, which condenses and revises the laws given earlier in the Pentateuch. Thus its name, *Deuteronomy*, means "second law." Chronicles and 2 Maccabees also condense and supplement material found in other books.

Sometimes God expanded on a previous work. This happened with Jeremiah. There was an original, shorter edition that was burned by King Jehoiakim, but God inspired a new edition that contained the original material as well as much new material (Jer. 36).

God did something similar in the deuterocanonical period. He inspired expanded editions of Daniel and Esther. The first includes three additional sections. One ("The Song of the Three Young Men") is a hymn sung by Daniel's companions. The other two ("Susannah" and "Bel and the Dragon") display Daniel's wisdom and show how God delivered him. In addition, the expanded edition of Esther includes sections that bring out more clearly the role of God. (The Hebrew edition, strikingly, doesn't contain explicit references to God.)

OTHER ANCIENT WRITINGS

The books of the Bible weren't the only ones written in ancient Israel. There were many others. Some are even considered canonical in Eastern non-Catholic churches. These include:

- *The Prayer of Manasseh*, a prayer of repentance attributed to one of Judah's kings;
- *1 Esdras*, which recounts the return of Jews following the Babylonian Exile;
- *3 Maccabees,* which deals with the situation of Jews in Egypt;
- *Psalm 151*, a psalm found in some versions of the Greek Old Testament.

Other influential works were also written during this time. They include:

- *1 Enoch,* a series of visions and narratives connected to the biblical patriarch Enoch; this work was influential enough to be quoted in the New Testament (Jude 14–15);

- *Jubilees*, a retelling of Genesis and part of Exodus;
- *The Apocalypse of Zephaniah,* which presents non-canonical visions of heaven and hell;
- *The Psalms of Solomon*, a collection of hymns.

The fact that these books weren't included in the Bible, despite their popularity in ancient times, shows the important role the Catholic Church would play in showing us which books belong in the canon of Scripture.

OLD TESTAMENT SOURCES

Tradition was an essential means for passing down information, especially in books like Genesis, which deals with the period before Israel was a kingdom.

It continued to be important as history progressed. Israel remained a largely oral culture, and tradition was the normal way information passed from person to person. Many of the Old Testament prophets did not even write books.

We know, for example, that in the time of Elijah, the 800s B.C., there were at least 100 prophets of the Lord (1 Kings 18:4), but we have no record of them writing books. Thus, they are what are known as *oral prophets*.

Elijah himself was an oral prophet. There is no indication he ever wrote a book, but he is considered the most prominent Old Testament prophet, and during the ministry of Jesus he appeared on the Mount of Transfiguration, where Moses and Elijah represented the law and the prophets and how they testify to Jesus (Luke 9:30–31; cf. 24:27).

Other oral prophets include Elisha (1 Kings 19:16), Micaiah (2 Kings 22:13), Hanani (2 Chron. 16:7), and Jahaziel (2 Chron. 20:14). Some oral prophets were women.

These included Moses' sister, Miriam (Exod. 15:20), Deborah (Judg. 4:4), and Huldah (2 Kings 22:14).

The existence of oral prophets illustrates how God continued to give his word in oral form and not exclusively in Scripture. On the other hand, some prophets did write books, though they are not part of the Bible.

Samuel wrote a book on the rights and duties of a king (1 Sam. 10:25). He also wrote one, apparently of a historical nature, known as the *Chronicles of Samuel the Seer* (1 Chron. 29:29). Others who did this include Gad and Nathan (1 Chron. 29:29), Nathan (2 Chron. 9:29), and Shemaiah and Iddo (2 Chron. 12:15). These records presumably included information about the events of their times, as well as prophecies they received. Some wrote books that may have been more directly prophetic—that is, just the revelations they received. These include the prophets Ahijah the Shilonite and Iddo the Seer (2 Chron. 9:29).

Surprisingly, even some prophets who *did* write books of the Bible *also* wrote other works. Isaiah wrote a history of King Uzziah (2 Chron. 26:22), and Jeremiah wrote a second book of lamentations dealing with the death of Josiah (2 Chron. 35:25).

Besides books written by prophets, we know of other works, such as the *Book of the Wars of the Lord* (Num. 21:14) and the *Book of Jashar* (Josh. 10:12). Once the monarchy began, court records were kept, and Scripture mentions the *Chronicles of the Kings of Israel* (1 Kings 14:19), the *Chronicles of the Kings of Judah* (1 Kings 14:29), the *Chronicles of King David* (1 Chron. 27:24), and the *Acts of Solomon* (1 Kings 11:41).

These books are sometimes directly quoted in the Old Testament. Sometimes they are used as sources without being quoted. And sometimes the biblical writer refers the reader to them for further information. This means they were important, but the fact that they aren't in the Bible shows God didn't ultimately want them in the canon.

While the court records weren't divinely inspired, the ancient Hebrews would have seen the books by prophets—especially ones containing divine revelations—as containing the word of God. This serves as a caution against identifying the canon of Scripture too closely with God's word. God gave his word to men in many ways, and he chose only some of it to be included in the Bible.

CHANGING LANGUAGES

Abraham, as a man from "Ur of the Chaldeans" (Gen. 11:28), would have spoken one of the Mesopotamian languages common in that region, such as Akkadian.

However, when he moved to the promised land, his household needed to learn the language of the Canaanites. Abraham's descendants thus began to speak "the language of Canaan" (Isa. 19:18), and today we refer to the dialect they eventually developed as Hebrew.

In Egypt, Israelites including Moses would have learned Egyptian. They may have continued to use an early dialect of Hebrew in their own circles, but they certainly used it once they returned to the promised land. By about 1000 B.C., they were definitely speaking Hebrew.

A writing system for Hebrew developed that was based on the Proto-Sinaitic script. This alphabet also was used by the Phoenicians, who had an extensive trading network. Through them, it spread to the Greeks and Latins. Surprising as it may seem, our English alphabet is based on the same one as Hebrew.

One reason our alphabet looks so different is that the direction of writing flipped. Hebrew is written right to left, while English is left to right. This means some letters are reversed. The Hebrew equivalents of *r* and *q* are inverted, making them hard to recognize.

Modern Hebrew letters Resh *and* Qoph *("R" and "Q")*

Hebrew also didn't originally have vowels, only consonants. The Greeks introduced new letters for vowel sounds, but in Hebrew a system of small marks known as *vowel points* were introduced. These are dots or other small marks written above, below, or inside the consonants.

בְּרֵאשִׁית בָּרָא אֱלֹהִים אֵת הַשָּׁמַיִם וְאֵת הָאָרֶץ:
וְהָאָרֶץ הָיְתָה תֹהוּ וָבֹהוּ וְחֹשֶׁךְ עַל־פְּנֵי תְהוֹם וְרוּחַ אֱלֹהִים

First lines of Genesis in Hebrew

Most Old Testament books were written in Hebrew, but not all. In 587 B.C., the Babylonian king Nebuchadnezzar conquered Jerusalem and deported many, beginning the Babylonian Exile. As with previous migrations, this caused a language change. Since the international language in the Middle East was Aramaic, the Hebrews began learning it.

Hebrew and Aramaic are related and have many words in common. In both languages, for example, the word for king is *melek*. This made Aramaic easier for Hebrews to learn. But there also are differences. The Hebrew word for son is *ben*, but the Aramaic equivalent is *bar*. That's why in the New Testament St. Peter's birth name is Simon bar-Jona rather than Simon ben-Jona.

Hebrew and Aramaic aren't mutually intelligible. In 701 B.C., during the reign of King Hezekiah, the Assyrians threatened to conquer Jerusalem, and their envoy shouted the threats in Hebrew to the soldiers on Jerusalem's walls. Hezekiah's ambassadors asked the Assyrians to speak in the international language of Aramaic, lest the Hebrew troops be demoralized, but they refused to do so (2 Kings 18:26–27). By Jesus' day, Aramaic had become the normal language that Jews in Palestine spoke, and this transition had several effects. One is that Aramaic started to be used in Scripture. Significant portions of Ezra and Daniel were written in Aramaic (i.e., Ezra 4:8–6:8; 7:12–26; Dan. 2:4–7:28), and Tobit appears to have been written in Aramaic.

Hebrew continued to be used by some, and some later Old Testament books, such as Judith, Sirach, and Baruch, were written in Hebrew. However, Aramaic became more and more the normal spoken language.

Because ordinary people no longer knew Hebrew, they needed the scriptures translated for them. This resulted in Aramaic translations of the Old Testament known as the *targums*. These originated in the synagogues, where a lector would first read biblical passages in Hebrew and then translate them into Aramaic.

Another language change began in the 330s B.C., with Alexander the Great. His troops spoke different dialects of Greek, and these blended together to form a dialect known as *koinê* or "common" Greek. It's different from the classical Greek used by Homer and Plato. Later scholars were puzzled as to why the New Testament doesn't use classical Greek, and some speculated it used a special dialect that God created—a *Holy Ghost Greek*—but modern archaeological discoveries show it's written in *koinê,* the common form of Greek in the first century.

Ἐν ἀρχῇ ἐποίησεν ὁ θεὸς τὸν οὐρανὸν καὶ τὴν γῆν. ἡ δὲ γῆ ἦν ἀόρατος καὶ ἀκατασκεύαστος, καὶ σκότος

First lines of Genesis in Greek

Alexander's conquests made Greek a new international language, particularly in the West. It was even widely used in Rome, where the local language was Latin. Greek was so widespread that the New Testament authors wrote in it rather than other languages.

During his career, Alexander founded several cities, including Alexandria, Egypt. Its inhabitants spoke Greek rather than Egyptian, and after about 300 B.C. a major Jewish colony was established there. Many Jews also were living elsewhere outside the Holy Land—a phenomenon known as the *Dispersion* of the Jewish people among the nations (see Jas. 1:1). Most learned Greek in addition to whatever other languages they knew.

Consequently, a few Old Testament books were written in Greek. These include Wisdom, which was likely written at Alexandria, and 2 Maccabees.

The other Old Testament books also needed to be translated for Jews who didn't speak Hebrew or Aramaic. This led to a Greek translation known as the *Septuagint*. Its name comes from the Latin word for seventy (*septuaginta*), and scholars often use the Latin numeral seventy—LXX—as an abbreviation for it.

This is because, according to an ancient document known as the *Letter of Aristeas*, the translation was begun by a team of seventy-two Jewish scholars. The letter states that Pharaoh Ptolemy II (r. 285–245 B.C.) ordered a Greek translation of the Jewish law books—the Torah—for the Library of Alexandria. This became the core of the Septuagint, and later the other Old Testament books also were translated or composed in Greek. Today scholars think the *Letter of Aristeas* isn't entirely accurate, but it's likely the Septuagint was begun by the Greek-speaking Jewish colony at Alexandria, possibly during the reign of Ptolemy II and in connection with the Library of Alexandria.

JEWISH SECTS

By the end of the Old Testament era, a number of movements had developed in the Jewish community.

One was the Sadducees. This relatively small group was very influential and had support from wealthy, upper-class Jews. Sadducees didn't believe in an afterlife or angels. According to Luke, "the Sadducees say that there is no resurrection, nor angel, nor spirit" (Acts 23:8). They stressed free will and denied fate or predestination. Finally, the Sadducees rejected the oral traditions honored by the Pharisees.

The second group was the Pharisees. They gained prominence around 120 B.C., and they were more numerous than the Sadducees. The Jewish historian Josephus reports that around 2 B.C. there were 6,000 Pharisees.[4] They were popular with the ordinary people and believed in the immortality of the soul and the resurrection of the dead, as well as rewards and punishments in the afterlife. The Pharisees believed in both free will and predestination and sought to harmonize them. They maintained an extensive body of oral traditions, which they held to have been passed down from ancient times.

A third group not mentioned in the New Testament was the Essenes. They were separatists who had a dispute with the high priests after around 170 B.C. They objected to someone whom they referred to as "the Wicked Priest," and they believed he and his followers polluted the temple. They refused to participate in temple worship and expected the temple to be destroyed and replaced. Josephus says there were about 4,000 Essenes.[5] Most scholars believe they had a community near the Dead Sea and wrote the Dead Sea Scrolls.

The Essenes believed in the afterlife and bodily resurrection as well as angels. They also believed in a strict form of predestination and practiced asceticism with some remaining celibate. They were hostile toward outsiders and believed all other Jews were disobeying God. They thought they were living in Last Days and that soon they would fight and win a war between the "sons of light" (i.e., the Essenes themselves) and the "sons of darkness."

Another war-oriented group was the Zealots. Josephus describes them as the fourth major group of Jews in his day. They violently opposed the Romans, who conquered the Holy Land in 63 B.C. and installed Herod the Great as a client king. The Zealots passionately wanted to overthrow Roman rule, and they played a key role in starting the Great Jewish Revolt in A.D. 66, which led to the destruction of the temple.

There were smaller sects also. The Jewish philosopher Philo mentions an ascetic group known as the *Therapeutae*, who practiced healing. However, most Jews weren't members of one of these elite groups; they were ordinary, uneducated peasants who were known as the *people of the land* (Hebrew, *am ha-aretz*).

The only group that was strong enough to survive after the Great Jewish Revolt was the Pharisees, and their movement developed into modern rabbinic Judaism.

HOW THE OLD TESTAMENT CANON DEVELOPED

By the first century A.D., the books of the Old Testament had been written, but how did the canon form? Why were some like Ezekiel and Esther included while others like *1 Enoch* and *Jubilees* were not?

Some claim the decisions were made by a gathering of 120 Jewish sages known as the *Great Assembly*, which was founded after the Babylonian Exile by Ezra around 444 B.C.

In the A.D. 200s, rabbinical sages attributed all kinds of decisions to the Great Assembly, including the Old Testament canon. However, we have no contemporary records of the Great Assembly and no documents it issued. The earliest claims are around 600 years later, and modern scholars doubt it did the things claimed or that it even existed. It looks like the rabbis—the intellectual descendants of the Pharisees— attributed their own views to the legendary body to give them antiquity.

Another view holds that the priests made the decisions and kept an archive of the sacred books in the temple. Anything in this collection was canonical; anything that wasn't was not.

This view is mere speculation and is not backed up by the evidence. We know the Torah was kept at the temple (2 Kings 22:8–20), but we don't have a record of an official archive of the scriptures there. It would be surprising if there was, for the prophets were very critical of how the temple was run. Also, the Sadducees appear to have rejected many books of Scripture, and they were closely associated with the temple.

A third view holds that there were two canons in circulation—the *Palestinian canon* and the *Alexandrian canon*. The first contained the protocanonical Old Testament books written in Hebrew (with some Aramaic passages). It was used in Palestine and represented the pure Old Testament. Outside Palestine, where Greek was common, the broader, Alexandria-based Septuagint collection was used. Advocates of this theory sometimes claim that the Palestinian canon was finalized around A.D. 90 at a meeting known as the *Council of Jamnia.*

This view was common in the nineteenth century, but twentieth-century scholarship destroyed it. There was disagreement even in Palestine regarding which books were considered to be Scripture, and some didn't consider the canon closed.

All Jews—and even the Samaritans—accepted the Pentateuch. These five books were foundational for the Jewish faith, and they were considered by far the most important books. Even those who accepted other works as Scripture considered these preeminent.

The Samaritans accepted *only* the Pentateuch as Scripture, and we have no evidence they ever accepted other books as such. It thus appears they had a closed and very limited canon. The same may be true of the Sadducees. The Church Fathers state that the Sadducees accepted only the Pentateuch.[6]

As Luke notes (Acts 23:8), they didn't accept the resurrection of the dead, which is unambiguously attested in passages outside the Pentateuch, like Daniel 12:1–2 (cf. Isa. 26:19; Ezek. 37:1–14). It's hard to see how they would have included these books in their canon if they disbelieved in the resurrection. Also, when the Sadducees challenge Jesus about the resurrection (Matt. 22:23–33), he cites the Pentateuch (Exod. 3:6) instead of the more obvious passages outside it—likely because they didn't accept the other books.

The Sadducees thus appear not to have accepted all of the books of the Hebrew Old Testament and may have had a canon limited to the Pentateuch.

This wasn't the case for the Pharisees. They accepted additional books that corresponded roughly to the proto-canonical books found in Jewish Bibles today. However, the boundaries of this collection were still somewhat fuzzy.

Those who say the Council of Jamnia closed their canon around A.D. 90 admit it wasn't closed before this time—and that's true—but it wasn't fixed until later.

There was no "council" at Jamnia. Councils are temporary gatherings that meet for a time and then disband. They are a Christian rather than a Jewish institution. What actually happened was that during the Jewish War of the A.D. 60s, a sage named Johanan ben Zakkai obtained permission from Roman authorities to establish a rabbinical school in Jamnia (also known as Jabneh or Yavneh). After the war, the Jewish ruling council relocated there.

We don't have records saying the sages of Jamnia attempted to close the canon. In fact, rabbinic writings such as the Mishnah and the Palestinian and Babylonian Talmuds reveal there was a diversity of opinion among the sages about certain books. Some rabbis opposed the scriptural status of six books—Ruth, Esther, Proverbs, Ecclesiastes, Song of Solomon, and Ezekiel. By contrast, some quoted Sirach as a book of Scripture, though it was eventually excluded.[7] This uncertainty continued for several hundred years into the Christian era, and the Jewish canon wasn't closed until the third or fourth century.

The discovery of the Dead Sea Scrolls revealed the Essenes had an even larger collection of scriptures. They appear to have included all of the protocanonicals except Esther. The likely reason is that the Jewish liturgical calendar was extremely important to them, and Esther conflicted with their understanding of the calendar. Hebrew and Aramaic copies of books like Sirach and Tobit also were discovered among the Dead Sea Scrolls.

The sect had a large library of other materials, and many probably weren't regarded as Scripture. However, several factors—such as whether they were quoted as Scripture, had commentaries based on them, or were treated as prophetic texts—have led scholars to argue that some of them were. These include *1 Enoch*, *Jubilees*, and a document known as the *Temple Scroll*.

The Septuagint tradition, which included not only the protocanonicals but also seven additional books: Tobit, Judith, 1–2 Maccabees, Baruch, Sirach, and Wisdom as well as expanded editions of Daniel and Esther, this tradition also had fuzzy boundaries. Some editions of the Septuagint included additional books such as *1–2 Esdras*, *3–4 Maccabees*, and the *Prayer of Manasseh*.

There were thus at least five major canonical traditions in the first century:

- The Samaritan tradition
- The Sadducee tradition
- The Pharisee tradition
- The Essene tradition
- The Septuagint tradition

None except the Samaritan tradition, and possibly the Sadducee tradition, represented a closed, fixed list of Scripture. Instead, they were open and had fuzzy boundaries, and this fuzziness would persist for centuries into the Christian age.

Finally, there were books in circulation that were presented as divine revelation, though we can't show that they were part of one of these established canonical traditions. They include works like the *Apocalypse of Zephaniah*. Some modern authors dismiss them as if nobody in the ancient world regarded them as Scripture, but this doesn't fit the evidence. That these books survived indicates they were popular. If they hadn't been, not enough copies would have been made for them to survive. An individual copy had only a small chance of surviving the ages, so there must have been many copies in circulation. But if a popular book presented itself as prophecy—like the *Apocalypse of Zephaniah*—this is strong evidence at least some ancient Jews considered it Scripture.

400 SILENT YEARS?

Many in the Protestant community discount books not found in their version of the Old Testament on the grounds that there were "400 silent years" between Malachi and the ministry of Jesus.

This claim is bolstered by the assertion that there were no prophets in this period. The implication is that without the divine inspiration given to prophets books of Scripture couldn't be written.

There are several problems with this assertion. One is that it isn't clear that all the books in the Protestant Old Testament were written before 400 B.C. Even among conservative Protestant scholars, a significant body of opinion holds that some were written much closer to the time of Christ.

Another problem is that an author doesn't have to be a prophet to write Scripture. While all of the biblical authors were divinely inspired, this didn't mean that they functioned in society as prophets. Psalms and Proverbs attribute many passages to David and Solomon, but they were kings, not prophets. The truth is, we don't know who wrote many Old Testament books, including all the historical ones (Joshua to 2 Chronicles), and it's just supposition to claim that they were written by prophets. We also have no evidence that New Testament authors like Mark and Luke ever received prophetic revelations.

But even if we were to grant that one had to be a prophet to author Scripture, we don't have evidence that the gift of prophecy was absent in this period. Sometimes advocates of the "four hundred silent years" appeal to passages like 1 Maccabees 4:46 and 9:27 to support the claim that there were no prophets in this era, but these passages don't show this.

The first describes how, around 164 B.C., Judah Maccabee and his men debated what to do about an altar the Gentiles had defiled. They tore it down and stored "the stones in a convenient place on the temple hill until there should come a prophet to tell what to do with them." The second refers to a few years later, when "there was great distress in Israel, such as had not been since the time that prophets ceased to appear among them."

These passages indicate that in the 160s B.C. there were no prophets functioning, but that doesn't mean that God *never* gave prophecies between Malachi and John the Baptist or that Jews of the period didn't *expect* new prophets. First Maccabees 4:46 shows they did when it says that they set aside the altar stones until "there should come a prophet to tell them what to do with them." Similarly, 1 Maccabees 14:41 states that in 140 B.C. Simon Maccabee was made ruler of the people "until a trustworthy prophet should arise," again indicating an expectation of further prophets, including the possibility of one arriving in the reign of Simon Maccabee.

The absence of prophets in the time of the Maccabees was a temporary event, and it wasn't unprecedented. There were similar lulls in prophetic activity in other periods. First Samuel 3:1 reveals that when the prophet Samuel was a boy "the word of the Lord was rare in those days; there was no frequent vision." Yet later in his life, when Samuel anointed Saul as king, there was a band of prophets that met Saul on the road, and he himself was overcome by the Spirit and began to prophesy. Thus, it became a proverb, "Is Saul also among the prophets?" (see 1 Sam. 10:9–12).

Another prophetic lull is mentioned during the Babylonian Exile. Psalm 74, which records the destruction of the temple (vv. 4–7), says, "We do not see our signs; there is no longer any prophet" (v. 9). Similarly, Lamentations 2:9 describes events following the destruction of the temple by saying Zion's "prophets obtain no vision from the Lord." Yet, neither passage indicates that the age of Old Testament prophecy was closed, for prophets like Jeremiah, Ezekiel, and Daniel were active during the Exile. Neither do these prophetic lulls indicate Scripture couldn't be written, for both passages are part of Scripture!

Even in a prophetic lull, God could give revelation, as in the case of the previous two passages. Similarly, in the time of the Maccabees, Judah Maccabee himself received a revelation (2 Macc. 15:11–16), though he didn't function as a formal prophet.

The Jewish historian Josephus reports that the Maccabean high priest John Hyrcanus, who ruled between 134 and 104 B.C., had "the gift of prophecy. For so closely was he in touch with the deity that he was never ignorant of the future; thus, he foresaw and predicted that his two elder sons would not remain at the head of affairs."[8]

In the New Testament, we learn that the holy priest Simeon had received a revelation from the Holy Spirit "that he should not see death before he had seen the Lord's Christ" (Luke 2:26), and we meet the "prophetess Anna, the daughter of Phanuel, of the tribe of Asher," who decades before the ministry of John the Baptist prophesied concerning Jesus "to all who were looking for the redemption of Jerusalem" (Luke 2:36, 38).

The readiness of people to accept John the Baptist and Jesus as a prophet (Matt. 21:11, 26; Mark 11:32; Luke 20:6; 24:19) also testifies to belief in ongoing prophecy.

According to Jesus' contemporary, the Jewish philosopher Philo (ca. 20 B.C.–ca. A.D. 50), "the sacred scriptures testify in the case of every good man, that he is a prophet; for a prophet says nothing of his own, but everything which he says is strange and prompted by someone else"—i.e., God—and that "the wise man alone . . . is a sounding instrument of God's voice, being struck and moved to sound in an invisible manner by him."[9] He also reported that he himself "was accustomed frequently to be seized with a certain divine inspiration"[10] and to have "suddenly become full, ideas being, in an invisible manner, showered upon me, and implanted in me from on high."[11]

After the ministry of Jesus, other Jewish prophets continued to appear, including the peasant Jesus, son of Ananus, who began in A.D. 62 to prophesy the destruction of Jerusalem and its temple.[12] Even false prophets such as Bar-Jesus (Acts 13:6) depended on belief in ongoing prophecy.

The evidence indicates that there was no belief at the time that prophecy had ceased. Instead, the attitude of the time was that "in every generation she [wisdom] passes into holy souls and makes them friends of God, and prophets" (Wis. 7:27).

2

The Word of God Incarnate

THE WORD BECOMES FLESH

The next phase of God's plan began with a series of personal revelations.

The first occurred when the angel Gabriel appeared to the elderly priest Zechariah and told him that—despite his advanced age and his wife's barrenness—they would have a son who would have a prophetic ministry leading many to repent. Zecharaiah didn't believe the message and demanded proof ("How shall I know this?"). Gabriel replied that he would be mute until the child was born, which is what happened (Luke 1:5–23).

The second revelation occurred when Gabriel again appeared, this time to the Virgin Mary, and announced she would bear "the Son of the Most High." Mary believed the prophecy but asked how it would be fulfilled. Since she was betrothed to and thus legally married to Joseph at the time, her question suggests she wasn't planning on a normal marriage and intended to remain a virgin. Gabriel replied that the Holy Spirit would bring about the conception without a human father, thus revealing the child as the Son of God (Luke 1:26–35).

When Joseph learned Mary was pregnant, he planned to divorce her quietly rather than publicly shaming her, but an angel appeared in a dream and let him know the divine origin of the pregnancy. Joseph thus agreed to take Mary as his wife (Matt. 1:18–25).

Elizabeth gave birth, as promised, to a son who was named John, and his father Zecharaiah was again able to speak. He was filled with the Holy Spirit and prophesied, declaring the ministry that John would have (Luke 1:57–79). As an adult, he would be known as John the Baptist because of the baptisms he performed.

When Mary gave birth to Jesus, local shepherds received an apparition of angels announcing the good news, and they came to see the baby (Luke 2:6–20). Then, when Jesus was taken to the temple for the customary offerings, his parents encountered the priest Simeon and the prophetess Anna, both of whom received revelations concerning Jesus (Luke 2:22–38).

When Jesus was between one and two years old, Magi came from the East to pay homage to him as the newborn king of the Jews, but their arrival alarmed Herod the Great, and angels warned both them and Joseph to flee from Herod, who would seek to kill the child. When Herod died, an angel again appeared to Joseph to let him know it was safe to return (Matt. 2:1–23).

All these revelations disclosed God's word in oral form—not in writing. They were passed down by oral tradition, and it would be decades before any were recorded in books of Scripture, reminding us of the role that oral tradition plays in God's plan.

God's word takes other forms, and the prologue to John's Gospel reveals the most fundamental:

In the beginning was the Word, and the Word was with

God, and the Word was God. He was in the beginning with God; all things were made through him, and without him was not anything made that was made.

And the Word became flesh and dwelt among us, full of grace and truth; we have beheld his glory, glory as of the only Son from the Father (John 1:1–3, 14).

Jesus is the ultimate Word of God. These verses invoke the first line of Genesis ("In the beginning God created the heavens and the earth," Gen. 1:1), calling us back to the moment of creation. They reveal that the Word was not a created reality. There was never a time when he did not exist, for he was there "in the beginning."

The verses also recall how Genesis pictures God creating the world by speaking—by his Word ("And God said, 'Let there be light'; and there was light," Gen. 1:3). The Word was God's creative agency, through whom every created thing was made, "and without him was not anything made that was made."

A man's word reveals his mind—who he is—and in this way Jesus reveals who the Father is. As he later would say, "He who has seen me has seen the Father" (John 14:9). Thus, Jesus "is the image of the invisible God" (Col. 1:15).

As an uncreated Person who perfectly mirrors the Father, Jesus is a divine Person, so John tell us not only that "the Word was with God" but also that "the Word was God."

Jesus became part of the world he created. "The Word became flesh and dwelt among us." By being born of the Virgin Mary, Jesus became part of the human family.

JESUS PREACHES THE WORD

With time, both Jesus and John the Baptist grew to adulthood. St. Luke tells us that John the Baptist began his ministry "in the fifteenth year of the reign of Tiberius Caesar,"—which was in A.D. 29—and "he went into all the region about the Jordan, preaching a baptism of repentance for the forgiveness of sins" (Luke 3:1–3). His message was, "Repent, for the kingdom of heaven is at hand" (Matt. 3:2). He also prophesied that "he who is coming after me is mightier than I, whose sandals I am not worthy to carry; he will baptize you with the Holy Spirit and with fire" (Matt. 3:11).

Jesus began his ministry at "about thirty years of age" (Luke 3:23). He came to John and was baptized in the Jordan "to fulfill all righteousness" (Matt. 3:15). This happened so that Jesus "might be revealed to Israel" (John 1:31). Then "the heavens were opened and he saw the Spirit of God descending like a dove, and alighting on him; and lo, a voice from heaven, saying, 'This is my beloved Son, with whom I am well pleased'" (Matt. 3:16–17). Jesus then prepared for ministry by spending forty days fasting in the wilderness.

When he returned, he began preaching God's word to the people. Like John, Jesus preached, "Repent, for the kingdom of heaven is at hand" (Matt. 4:17). But there was a difference between his teaching Jesus and all others. As the Son of God, Jesus could settle matters by his divine authority. Because of this, "he taught them as one who had authority, and not as the scribes" (Mark 1:22).

We see him doing this in the Sermon on the Mount (Matt. 5–7), his major ethical discourse. In it, Jesus upends common interpretations of Old Testament Law, saying, "You have heard . . ." and then revealing the true understanding by his own authority: "But I say . . ." He doesn't appeal to other authorities. It's his own authority that settles the matter.

In making these declarations, he warns the crowd, "Think not that I have come to abolish the law and the prophets; I have come not to abolish them but to fulfill them" (Matt. 5:17)—that is, to bring out their true meaning. He thus reveals that the laws don't apply just to outward behavior but to our hearts: "You have heard that it was said, 'You shall not commit adultery.' But I say to you that everyone who looks at a woman lustfully has already committed adultery with her in his heart" (Matt. 5:27–28).

The priority of the heart is made clear when Jesus discusses Old Testament purity laws. According to the Law of Moses, eating certain foods would make one ritually unclean, and by Jesus' day the Pharisees had extended this to saying that if one ate with unwashed hands it would make one unclean. Jesus responded by saying that, in extending this commandment beyond what God's word said, the Pharisees "leave the commandment of God, and hold fast the tradition of men" (Mark 7:8).

He also indicated that what was truly important was not ritual purity but moral purity, declaring:

> "Do you not see that whatever goes into a man from outside cannot defile him, since it enters, not his heart but his stomach, and so passes on?" (Thus, he declared all foods clean.) And he said, "What comes out of a man is what defiles a man. For from within, out of the heart of man, come evil thoughts, fornication, theft, murder, adultery, coveting, wickedness, deceit, licentiousness, envy, slander, pride, foolishness. All these evil things come from within, and they defile a man" (Mark 7:18–23).

Jesus indicated that the true concern of Old Testament Law wasn't the external matters that it regulated but the disposition of the heart, which needed to be one of love. When asked to name the greatest commandment, he replied:

"'You shall love the Lord your God with all your heart, and with all your soul, and with all your mind.' This is the great and first commandment. And a second is like it, 'You shall love your neighbor as yourself.' On these two commandments depend all the law and the prophets" (Matt. 22:37–40).

In addition to his moral teaching, Jesus taught many things in parables. These were brief stories that communicated spiritual realities. His most famous one is the Parable of the Sower (Mark 4:3–8). In it, a farmer scatters seeds that fall on different types of ground, producing different results. Seed that falls on a path is eaten by birds; seed that falls on rocky ground shoots up quickly but withers because it has no roots; seed that falls among thorns is choked by weeds; and seed that falls on good ground yields an abundant harvest.

Jesus means this parable—which is simply agricultural on the surface—to be taken in a deeper, spiritual sense. He explains (Mark 4:14–20) that seed represents the word of God, and the types of soil it falls on represent the ways people receive it: some never respond to the word because of the action of the devil; others receive it with joy but lose faith because it isn't firmly rooted in their hearts; others believe but don't bear spiritual fruit because they're choked by the cares of life; and others receive it properly and bear great spiritual fruit. Jesus thus says, "Take heed then how you hear" (Luke 8:18)—that is, make sure you respond to the word of God the right way.

Jesus also made prophecies. On a number of occasions, he predicted his death at the hands of the Jewish authorities and his subsequent resurrection from the dead (see, e.g., Mark 8:31–32; 9:9, 12, 31; 10:33–34).

When Jesus first predicted these, Peter rebuked him (Mark 8:32). The prediction startled Peter, because he had just confessed Jesus as the Messiah, or the Christ (Mark 8:29), and the popular understanding of the Messiah was that he would be a victorious military leader who would expel the Romans and restore the Davidic monarchy. How could a triumphant Messiah be killed by the Jewish authorities? In the popular understanding of the day, the idea made no sense.

Jesus' statements that he would rise "on the third day" also perplexed his disciples. All Jews except the Sadducees expected the dead to rise at the end of the world. Thus, Martha told Jesus that her brother Lazarus would be raised then: "I know that he will rise again in the resurrection at the Last Day" (John 11:24). Nobody expected the Messiah to die—much less be resurrected three days later—so the disciples didn't know what to think. Instead, "they kept the matter to themselves, questioning what the rising from the dead meant" (Mark 9:10).

Jesus also didn't expect the Romans to be expelled from Israel. On the contrary, he foresaw a war with the Romans, with Jewish forces being defeated and the temple destroyed. This became clear to the disciples one day as they were leaving the temple and commenting on its great size and beauty. There was a saying among later rabbis that "he who has not seen the temple of Herod has never seen a beautiful building."[13] The disciples thus were shocked to hear Jesus say, "Do you see these great buildings? There will not be left here one stone upon another, that will not be thrown down" (Mark 13:2).

The disciples were naturally curious, and they asked him, "Tell us, when will this be, and what will be the sign when these things are all to be accomplished?" (Mark 13:4). Jesus replied with his lengthiest prophecy, in which he described a coming time of trouble leading up to the destruction of the temple. He indicated it would happen soon: "Truly, I say to you, this generation will not pass away before all these things take place" (Mark 13:30). The Great Jewish Revolt began in A.D. 66, and the Romans destroyed the temple in August of 70, less than forty years after Jesus' prophecy.

Jesus also gave prophecies about the end of the world, but he tended to frame them in the form of parables, perhaps because the final end is beyond our present ability to imagine (cf. Rom. 8:18; 2 Cor. 4:17; 1 John 3:2). His parables about the end of the world include the Parable of the Ten Virgins (Matt. 25:1–13), of the Talents (Matt. 25:14–30), and of the Sheep and the Goats (Matt. 25:31–46)—the last focusing on Christ's role as the judge of the living and the dead.

In giving all of these teachings, Jesus was going beyond what was written in Scripture in his day. He was creating new oral traditions that, as the word of God, would be fully authoritative for the Christian community even before they were put in the books of the New Testament.

JESUS FOUNDS HIS CHURCH

As he preached the word of God, Jesus was also founding his Church. The Greek term for church, *ekklesia*, means "assembly," and Jesus began assembling followers around him. One way he did this was by performing miracles—signs from God that validated his message.

It was sometimes possible for a prophet to gain a hearing without miracles. John the Baptist was regarded as a prophet (Mark 11:32) though he never performed a sign (John 10:41). But miracles were normally important to validate the role of a prophet. In fact, if one proclaimed a sign and it failed to happen, it was evidence he was a false prophet (Deut. 18:21–22).

The signs Jesus performed, such as healings and exorcisms, were important for validating his ministry. Early in his career, the Jewish leader Nicodemus came to him and said, "Rabbi, we know that you are a teacher come from God; for no one can do these signs that you do, unless God is with him" (John 3:2). Jesus himself commented on the people's reaction to the miracles, saying, "Unless you see signs and wonders you will not believe" (John 4:48). Later, he appealed to them as proof for his critics, saying, "even though you do not believe me, believe the works, that you may know and understand that the Father is in me and I am in the Father" (John 10:38).

People began following Jesus as soon as he was baptized, and John declared him "the Lamb of God, who takes away the sin of the world" (John 1:29). Some of John the Baptist's own disciples began following Jesus (John 1:35–51). Jesus also began to invite individual men to follow him (Matt. 4:18–22; 9:9–13). Eventually, after spending a night in prayer, he selected twelve of his followers whom he commissioned as apostles—a term meaning "delegates" or "envoys" (Luke 6:13–16). These twelve became the first leaders of his Church.

With time, he appointed one of them—St. Peter—as the leader of the Twelve, telling him, "you are Peter, and on this rock I will build my Church, and the powers of death shall not prevail against it. I will give you the keys of the kingdom of heaven, and whatever you bind on earth shall be bound in heaven, and whatever you loose on earth shall be loosed in heaven" (Matt. 16:18–19).

In the Old Testament, the key of the kingdom was held by an official in the royal court—the chief steward who managed the royal household on the king's behalf. He had "on his shoulder the key of the house of David; he shall open, and none shall shut; and he shall shut, and none shall open" (Isa. 22:22).

Jesus—as the New David—applied this image to Peter and made him the chief steward of his new kingdom. Since this kingdom was spiritual rather than political, Peter didn't have the ability to open or close the doors of an earthly palace. He had the ability to bind and loose in a spiritual sense, so that his rulings would be backed up by God himself. Thus, Jesus says, "whatever you bind on earth shall be bound in heaven, and whatever you loose on earth shall be loosed in heaven."

This language is unfamiliar today, but it was well known then. As the *Jewish Encyclopedia* notes, binding and loosing was a "rabbinical term for 'forbidding and permitting.'" It explains:

> The power of binding and loosing was always claimed by the Pharisees. Under Queen Alexandra, the Pharisees, says Josephus (*Jewish War* 1:5:2), "became the administrators of all public affairs so as to be empowered to banish and readmit whom they pleased, as well as to loose and to bind." This does not mean that, as the learned men, they merely decided what, according to the law, was forbidden or allowed, but that they possessed and exercised the power of tying or untying a thing by the spell of their divine authority, just as they could, by the power vested in them, pronounce and revoke an anathema upon a person. The various schools had the power "to bind and to loose"; that is, to forbid and to permit (*Hag.* 3b); and they could bind any day by declaring it a fast-day (*Meg. Ta'an. 22.; Ta'an. 12a; Yer. Ned. 1: 36c, d*). This power and authority,

vested in the rabbinical body of each age or in the Sanhedrin, received its ratification and final sanction from the celestial court of justice (*Sifra, Emor, 9.; Mak. 23b*).

IN THE NEW TESTAMENT

In this sense, Jesus, when appointing his disciples to be his successors, used the familiar formula (Matt. 16:19, 18:18). By these words he virtually invested them with the same authority that he found belonging to the scribes and Pharisees who "bind heavy burdens and lay them on men's shoulders, but will not move them with one of their fingers"; that is, "loose them," as they have the power to do (Matt. 23:2–4) (s.v., "Binding and Loosing").

Jesus thus gave Peter the ability to establish laws for the Christian community. He later shared this authority with the other apostles. When discussing how to deal with a Christian who has sinned against a fellow believer, Jesus said:

If your brother sins against you, go and tell him his fault, between you and him alone. If he listens to you, you have gained your brother. But if he does not listen, take one or two others along with you, that every word may be confirmed by the evidence of two or three witnesses. If he refuses to listen to them, tell it to the church; and if he refuses to listen even to the church, let him be to you as a Gentile and a tax collector. Truly, I say to you, whatever you bind on earth shall be bound in heaven, and whatever you loose on earth shall be loosed in heaven (Matt. 18:15–18).

Jesus counsels settling matters privately if possible, but if the fellow Christian refuses to listen even to the Church then he is to be treated as a Gentile and tax collector—that is, an outsider. He is to be excommunicated. Jesus assures them this decision will be ratified in heaven because of the power of binding and loosing. The ability to exercise Church discipline, therefore, is included in this power.

While Jesus shared the power of binding and loosing with the apostles more generally, it was only Peter to whom he gave the keys. Peter's unique role is also stressed in the other Gospels.

In Luke, when a dispute breaks out about which of the disciples is the greatest, Jesus gives a three-part reply. First, he emphasizes they were not to be preoccupied with exercising lordship like "the kings of the Gentiles" but should take the attitude of servants in ministering to his flock (Luke 22:24–27). Second, he assures them they would each have a prominent place in his kingdom (Luke 22:28–30). And third, he says:

> Simon, Simon, behold, Satan demanded to have you, that he might sift you like wheat, but I have prayed for you that your faith may not fail; and when you have turned again, strengthen your brethren (Luke 22:31–32).

Jesus singled out Peter, giving him a special pastoral role with respect to the other apostles. He did the same thing after the Resurrection. In John's Gospel we read that, in the presence of the other disciples, Jesus said to him:

> "Simon, son of John, do you love me more than these?" He said to him, "Yes, Lord; you know that I love you." He said to him, "Feed my lambs" (John 21:15).

Jesus repeats the question twice more—so the conversation mirrors Peter's three denials of Jesus (see John 18:15–27)—and each time when Peter reaffirms his love for Jesus, Jesus tells him to care for his flock. Notice that Jesus has asked Peter if he loves him "more than these"—that is, more than the other disciples who are present. The disciples form part of the flock Jesus directs Peter to care for, again giving him a special pastoral role.

From the passages dealing with Jesus' Church, we can learn several things:

- He is establishing a single church. Jesus speaks of "my Church," not "my churches" (Matt. 16:18).
- This Church will never pass out of existence, for "the power of death shall not prevail against it" (Matt. 16:18).
- It will be built in a special way on Peter, who has a unique role among the other apostles (Matt. 16:18–19; Luke 22:31–32; John 21:15).
- Its leaders will have the power to bind and loose—that is, to make divinely-backed rules for the community—and to include or exclude members (Matt. 16:19; 18:17–18).

This means that when we look for Jesus' Church today, it must have these characteristics. It is not an "invisible" church that is just the spiritual union of all believers. It's a single body that has existed since the first century that has leaders, laws, and identifiable members and that is built on Peter in a special way.

The only church that has all those characteristics is the Catholic Church.

After establishing his Church, Jesus went on to empower it by his death on the cross. It was by this sacrifice that Jesus obtained the grace that flows both to individual believers and to his Church as a whole. Everything goes back to what Jesus did in this world–altering event.

Following the Crucifixion, Jesus rose from the dead and appeared to the disciples—proving that God has the power of resurrection and will one day raise all of us. Then, at the Ascension, Jesus returned to heaven where he would reign at the right hand of God the Father until the end of the world, when he will return to judge the living and the dead (see Luke 22:69; Acts 10:42; 1 Cor. 15:22–26).

Before he departed, Jesus gave his apostles the Great Commission, telling them:

> All authority in heaven and on earth has been given to me. Go therefore and make disciples of all nations, baptizing them in the name of the Father and of the Son and of the Holy Spirit, teaching them to observe all that I have commanded you; and lo, I am with you always, to the close of the age (Matt. 28:18–20).

Jesus gave them a worldwide teaching mission, assuring them that he would be with them and would guide his Church until the end of the world. He also promised the Holy Spirit would aid them. Even before the Crucifixion he had promised that "the Holy Spirit, whom the Father will send in my name, he will teach you all things, and bring to your remembrance all that I have said to you" (John 14:26); and, "When the Spirit of truth comes, he will guide you into all the truth" (John 16:13). As he was preparing to depart, he told them:

> It is written that the Christ should suffer and on the third day rise from the dead, and that repentance and forgiveness of sins should be preached in his name to all nations, beginning from Jerusalem. You are witnesses of these things. And behold, I send the promise of my Father

upon you; but stay in the city, until you are clothed with power from on high (Luke 24:46–49).

Thus, "he charged them not to depart from Jerusalem, but to wait for the promise of the Father, which, he said, 'you heard from me, for John baptized with water, but before many days you shall be baptized with the Holy Spirit'" (Acts 1:4–5). This empowering event took place fifty days after his resurrection, on Pentecost:

And suddenly a sound came from heaven like the rush of a mighty wind, and it filled all the house where they were sitting. And there appeared to them tongues as of fire, distributed and resting on each one of them. And they were all filled with the Holy Spirit and began to speak in other tongues, as the Spirit gave them utterance (Acts 2:2–4).

Under the leadership of Peter, the apostles preached to the international crowd of Jews who were in Jerusalem for the feast. From that time, Jesus and the Holy Spirit continued to guide his Church—the Catholic Church—and it grew dramatically.

TRADITION IN THE EARLY CHURCH

At first, the apostles conducted their teaching mission in a purely oral form. Peter preached a sermon on Pentecost. He did not issue a pamphlet.

By teaching orally, the apostles followed the example of Jesus, who didn't author any books, letters, or treatises. Only once do the Gospels mention Jesus writing, and that was with his finger on the ground (John 8:6, 8).

Communicating God's word orally was the most effective way to do it. The great majority of people—even in Israel—were illiterate. If you wanted to reach them with the message of salvation, it had to be orally.

This is why the New Testament describes Jesus and the apostles as *speaking* "the word" to people (e.g., Mark 2:2; 4:3; Acts 4:31; 6:2; 8:4; 11:19). It's also why the New Testament emphasizes the response of those who *hear* "the word" (e.g., Matt. 13:19; Luke 5:1; John 14:24; Acts 4:4; 10:44). St. Paul emphasizes the importance of oral proclamation for salvation by asking, rhetorically:

> But how are men to call upon him in whom they have not believed? And how are they to believe in him of whom they have never heard? And how are they to hear without a preacher? And how can men preach unless they are sent? As it is written, "How beautiful are the feet of those who preach good news!" (Rom. 10:14–15; cf. Isa. 52:7).

The fact the Christian message was given orally rather than in writing means it was a matter of Tradition. Certainly, parts of Christian teaching could be found in the Old Testament scriptures that pointed forward to Jesus, but the actual story of who he was, what he taught, and what he did for us by his cross and resurrection went beyond what had been written before. Tradition was the means by which the core message of our faith was preached.

This didn't mean *all* traditions were good, or that traditions should be accepted uncritically. During his ministry, Jesus had criticized the Pharisees for inventing new traditions that either went beyond or even contradicted God's commandments (Mark 7:1–13). He thus censured them for holding "the tradition of men" (Mark 7:8).

But traditions of men and Tradition handed down from Christ and his apostles are two different things! The first Christians recognized that the latter were not only binding on us but also essential for our faith and practice.

Consider the practice of St. Paul. Prior to the writing of the New Testament, he delivered the Christian message in the form of Tradition in the cities where he founded churches; and in the letters he later wrote to these churches, he instructed them on the proper attitude toward these traditions.

In 1 Corinthians 11:2, Paul tells his readers, "I commend you because you remember me in everything and maintain the traditions even as I have delivered them to you." He tells the Thessalonians, "Stand firm and hold to the traditions which you were taught by us, either by word of mouth or by letter" (2 Thess. 2:15). And he says, "Now we command you, brethren, in the name of our Lord Jesus Christ, that you keep away from any brother who is living in idleness and not in accord with the tradition that you received from us" (2 Thess. 3:6).

Some today don't like the concept of Tradition, and some modern Bible translations—especially in the Protestant community—try to obscure the fact that the New Testament speaks positively of tradition when it is passed down from Christ and the apostles. They do this by using the word *tradition* when Jesus criticizes the Pharisees but substituting another word—such as *teaching, ordinance, instruction,* or *truth*—when the New Testament praises Christian Tradition. This creates the false impression that tradition is a negative concept for the New Testament writers, but the underlying word in Greek (*paradosis*) is the same in all these passages.

Protestant translations that substitute another word for *tradition* in some or all the pro-tradition verses include the King James Version, the New International Version, the Good News Bible, the New Living Translation, and Young's Literal Translation. However, stopping to think for a moment about the fact that Christianity preached for years before the New Testament underscores the importance of Tradition for the Christian faith.

SCRIPTURE IN THE EARLY CHURCH

Jesus and the apostles did appeal to Scripture, and we should mention how the term was used in Jesus' day. The Greek word *graphê* originally just meant "writing," especially a brief piece of writing, but in Jewish and Christian contexts it came to mean "a holy writing," which is why it is often translated *scripture*.

Today we use this term to refer to the entire collection of holy books, saying things like, "Scripture contains the Old and the New Testaments." But in the first century, when the term was used in the singular, it normally referred to a *specific* book or passage. Thus, in Mark 12:10, Jesus says:

> Have you not read this scripture: "The very stone which the builders rejected has become the head of the corner; this was the Lord's doing, and it is marvelous in our eyes"?

The passage Jesus is quoting ("this scripture") is Psalm 118:22–23. By contrast, when people wanted to refer to *all* the holy writings as a group, they used the plural: "the scriptures." Thus, Jesus tells his Sadducee critics they are wrong, "because you know neither the scriptures nor the power of God" (Matt. 22:29).

Christians initially used this term for writings composed in the Old Testament period, for these were the only holy books at the time. Even when they began writing the books of the New Testament, they used "the scriptures" as a technical term for the earlier holy books. There are a few exceptions, such as when Paul refers to Luke's Gospel as "Scripture" (1 Tim. 5:18; see Luke 10:7) or when Peter lists Paul's letters alongside "the other scriptures" (2 Pet. 3:16), but referring to the books of the New Testament as "Scripture" really didn't catch on until the second century.

Jesus overturned many common religious ideas of in his day, but he didn't challenge the authority of Scripture. As the incarnate Word of God, he acknowledged the authority of the written word. Thus, he declared, "Not an iota, not a dot, will pass from the law until all is accomplished" (Matt. 5:17) and "scripture cannot be broken" (John 10:35).

Jesus saw his ministry as fulfilling Old Testament prophecy. At his triumphal entry, Jesus rode a young donkey in fulfillment of Zechariah 9:9 (see John 12:14–15) and when he was arrested, he declared, "All this has taken place, that the scriptures of the prophets might be fulfilled" (Matt. 26:56). Following the Resurrection, he spoke with two disciples and "beginning with Moses and all the prophets, he interpreted to them in all the scriptures the things concerning himself" (Luke 24:27).

THE SCRIPTURES JESUS ACCEPTED

If Jesus saw his ministry as the fulfillment of the Jewish scriptures, which ones did he have in mind?

In the Gospels, he commonly refers to "the law" and "the prophets" (e.g., Matt. 5:17; 7:12; 11:13). This was a common way of referring to the whole of the Old Testament, though it doesn't tell us which specific books he saw it including.

From the evidence of the Gospels, we can tell Jesus placed more emphasis on certain books than others. The ones he quoted from most were Psalms, Deuteronomy, Exodus, and Isaiah. Depending on how you reckon what counts as a passage, he quotes fifteen passages from the Psalms, eleven from Deuteronomy, eight from Exodus, and seven from Isaiah.

The large number of quotations from Deuteronomy and Exodus are to be expected, given the prominence of the Pentateuch in Jewish thought, and it's no surprise he also quotes from Genesis, Leviticus, and Numbers. When it comes to the prophets, Jesus quotes not only from Isaiah but also from Jeremiah and Daniel, as well as several minor prophets (Hosea, Jonah, Micah, Zechariah, and Malachi).[14]

Unfortunately, this doesn't allow us to say precisely which books he regarded as Scripture. The Gospels are only partial records of his words and actions, and the fact that they don't record him quoting a book doesn't mean that he *never* quoted it or didn't regard it as Scripture.

When scholars commonly believed there was a "Palestinian canon" that all Palestinian Jews accepted, it was easy to claim—that based on where he lived—Jesus simply accepted that canon. But as scholarship has advanced, it has become clear there were multiple, fuzzy canonical traditions even in Palestine.

It's likely Jesus accepted more books than the Sadducees. When they challenged him on the resurrection of the dead (Matt. 22:23–32), he conspicuously used Exodus 3:6 ("I am the God . . . of Abraham, the God of Isaac, and the God of Jacob") to prove that the dead will one day rise, though there are much clearer passages, such as Daniel 12:2 ("Many of those who sleep in the dust of the earth shall awake, some to everlasting life, and some to shame and everlasting contempt"). Jesus elsewhere cites Daniel as a prophet (Matt. 24:15) and quotes from his book (Matt. 24:30; 26:64). This indicates that Jesus treated Daniel as

Scripture, and he probably avoided using it with the Sadducees because they didn't accept it.

Some have tried to shed light on which books Jesus accepted by appealing to the languages he spoke. From various Aramaic words and phrases in the Gospels (see Mark 3:17; 5:41; 15:34), it's clear Jesus' daily language was Aramaic. When he quoted Scripture, he likely did so in Aramaic, based on the targums read in the synagogues. But it's also likely he used Hebrew, and some have argued he would have accepted a book as Scripture only if it was in Hebrew or Aramaic—excluding the deuterocanonical books.

There are several problems with this argument. One is that modern scholarship has shown most of the deutero-canonicals were actually written in Hebrew or Aramaic. These include Sirach, Tobit, Judith, Baruch, and 1 Maccabees, so language would not prevent Jesus from accepting them.

Also, Greek was an international language at the time, and it was spoken in Palestine. Modern scholars have taken seriously the idea that Jesus and his disciples may also have used Greek. In the Gospels, Jesus speaks to Gentiles on various occasions (e.g., Matt. 8:38–34; Mark 7:26), including the Roman governor (Matt. 27:11), who would not have known Aramaic; and a group of Greeks asked Philip to arrange an audience with Jesus for them (John 12:20–22).

We also have evidence that Jesus read and valued some of the deuterocanonicals. In the Lord's prayer, Jesus made a single petition contingent on our own actions rather than simply being a request made to God. He taught us to pray, "And forgive us our debts, as we also have forgiven our debtors" (Matt. 6:12), following it up by saying, "For if you forgive men their trespasses, your heavenly Father also will forgive you; but if you do not forgive men their trespasses, neither will your Father forgive your trespasses" (Matt. 6:14–15).

Scholars have noted that this expresses the same teaching found in Sirach 28:1–5 but not present elsewhere in the Old Testament. Thus, Sirach states, "Forgive your neighbor the wrong he has done, and then your sins will be pardoned when you pray" (Sir. 28:2).

THE SCRIPTURES THE NEW TESTAMENT AUTHORS ACCEPTED

If it's difficult to determine from the Gospels the precise books Jesus accepted, perhaps we can learn from the example of his followers. One would expect a teacher's disciples to hold the same views about Scripture as their master, and when we look at the writings of the New Testament we discover several things.

First, we can fill in some additional Old Testament books that are quoted by the New Testament authors. These include the historical books 1–2 Samuel and 1–2 Kings, the wisdom books Job and Proverbs, and the prophets Ezekiel, Joel, Amos, Nahum, Habakkuk, and Haggai.[15]

We have to be careful with quotations, however. Just because a work is quoted doesn't guarantee it was regarded as Scripture. Sometimes the New Testament authors quote from books they *don't* think are Scripture. Paul several times quotes from pagan sources. In Acts 17:28, he quotes from the pagan authors Epimenides and Aratus. In 1 Corinthians 15:33, he quotes from the Greek poet Menander, and in Titus 1:12, he again quotes Epimenides—even referring to him as a pagan "prophet" of the island of Crete.

If mere quotation isn't enough to show a book was considered Scripture, what is? Scholars have proposed certain tests. For example, if a quotation is introduced as "Scripture" (Greek, *graphê*; e.g., Mark 12:24) or with the formula "it is written" (e.g., Matt. 2:5), this is a strong sign that it was viewed as such. The same is indicated when an author attributes something to divine revelation, such as saying it was written "in the Spirit" (e.g., Matt. 22:43) or is attributed to a "prophet" or described as "prophecy" (e.g., Matt. 3:3). While these are strong indicators a work was considered Scripture, they aren't present with many of Old Testament quotations found in the New Testament.

Then there are books that aren't quoted at all. These include the historical books Judges, Ruth, Esther, Ezra, and Nehemiah; the wisdom books Song of Songs and Ecclesiastes; and the prophetic books Lamentations, Obadiah, and Zephaniah (though we can make an exception for the last two, since at the time they were part of *The Twelve*, and other prophets from that collection are quoted). This isn't to say these books *weren't* considered Scripture, just that we can't prove it from quotations in the New Testament.

What light can we shed on the question by looking at the language that the authors of the New Testament used? It's clear they had no problem with Greek, for all of the New Testament is written in that language. It's also clear that they didn't have a problem with the Septuagint. Around 90 percent of the Old Testament quotations found in the New Testament are based on the Septuagint, compared to around 10 percent based directly on the Hebrew text.[16]

Sometimes people ask if Jesus quoted the Septuagint. The answer is that we don't know. In the Greek text of the Gospels, the authors put the words of the Septuagint on his lips, but this doesn't prove the matter. Jesus ordinarily spoke Aramaic, and he likely quoted the Old Testament in Aramaic during his ministry. The Gospel writers are simply using the common Greek translation of those passages for the sake of their Greek–speaking readers. It's possible Jesus quoted the

Septuagint, especially when he was speaking to Gentiles, but we can't prove this from the Gospels.

What we can prove is that the New Testament authors—under the inspiration of the Holy Spirit—had no problem quoting the Septuagint. This is significant because the Septuagint included the deuterocanonical books, and the New Testament authors didn't issue warnings against regarding them—like the rest of the Septuagint—as Scripture.

Indeed, they appear to have been familiar with and to have valued them. For example, scholars have noted Paul's attack on idolatry in Romans 1:18–25 appears to be based on the book of Wisdom. Protestant scholar James D. G. Dunn comments:

> It is probable indeed that Paul was consciously modeling his exposition on the Wisdom of Solomon: the echoes of Wisdom's thought and language are quite marked in this section of the argument, particularly Wisdom 13–15, so much so that Romans 1:19–21 almost constitutes a summary of Wisdom 13:1–9 and Romans 1:23–25 of the powerful anti–idol polemic in Wisdom 13:10–15:19.[17]

Similarly, the author of Hebrews makes a clear allusion to 2 Maccabees. He describes a series of people in Old Testament times, saying "some were tortured, refusing to accept release, that they might rise again to a better life" (Heb. 11:35). This refers to an event discussed only in 2 Maccabees 7, where the pagan king Antiochus IV is having a mother and her seven sons tortured to death. Release is offered them if they will abandon their faith, but they refuse so they can obtain the resurrection to eternal life (2 Macc. 7:9, 11, 14, 23).

What the evidence in the Gospels and the rest of the New Testament allows us to say is that in the first century the early Christians had a collection of scriptures that broadly corresponded to the one found in the Septuagint tradition.

This is what one would expect since at the time there was no such thing as a Bible. The books later printed in Bibles were originally a library of scrolls, and there was no official list of which books belonged in the library. Different churches would have somewhat different collections, so the boundaries of the set were flexible.

It would be a mistake to assume the early Christians had a closed canon. Except for the Samaritans and perhaps the Sadducees, the idea of a known, fixed list of scriptures doesn't appear to have existed at this time. Instead, there was a variety of canonical traditions that had unclear boundaries. It would take centuries for these to solidify.

Certainly, the early Christians didn't believe that the list of inspired books was fixed. If they had, they wouldn't have written the books of the New Testament!

FROM PENTECOST TO THE NEW TESTAMENT

The book of Acts records the first decades of the Catholic Church, covering the period from around A.D. 33 to around A.D. 60. The New Testament books began to be written only toward the end of that period, so what happened before that?

Acts indicates that when St. Peter preached on Pentecost, around 3,000 people were converted (Acts 2:41). This was impressive growth for the Church. It also represented the first step in its spread throughout the nations, for many pilgrims had come to Jerusalem for the feast. Thus, when the Holy Spirit enabled the disciples to speak in tongues, the travelers heard what they were saying in their own languages, and it made a profound impression. St. Luke describes the crowd as including:

Parthians and Medes and Elamites and residents of Mesopotamia, Judea and Cappadocia, Pontus and Asia, Phrygia and Pamphylia, Egypt and the parts of Libya belonging to Cyrene, and visitors from Rome, both Jews and proselytes, Cretans and Arabians (Acts 2:9–11).

Many of these ancient names are unfamiliar today, but they represent a wide range of points in southern Europe, North Africa, and the Middle East. The fact that Luke specifically mentions there being "visitors from Rome, both Jews and proselytes" means some of the pilgrims came from the empire's capital, and these included both people who were born Jewish or who had converted to Judaism.

Luke spends a large portion of Acts building up to Paul's arrival in Rome, where a Christian community was waiting to meet him (Acts 28:14–15). It's likely Luke mentions these pilgrims here to show how Christianity originally reached Rome: they brought the Faith with them when they returned home.

Pilgrims from the other lands also returned home along with their new faith, so Jesus' words began to be fulfilled "that repentance and forgiveness of sins should be preached in his name to all nations, beginning from Jerusalem" (Luke 24:47).

Acts records Jesus making a similar statement just before the Ascension, telling the disciples: "You shall receive power when the Holy Spirit has come upon you; and you shall be my witnesses in Jerusalem and in all Judea and Samaria and to the end of the earth" (Acts 1:8). Scholars have long noted that this is the basic outline of Acts.

Though Galileans by birth, the apostles relocated to Jerusalem and made it the base of operations for their ongoing mission. This made sense. There were scattered believers in Jesus in many towns in Galilee and Judea, but if you wanted to preach the Faith effectively, it made sense to do it where the largest numbers of Jews were, and that was Jerusalem. Also, as the events of Pentecost showed them, the Faith would spread from Jerusalem, as Jews traveled back and forth to the city.

The apostles also performed miracles, which validated their message, and soon the number of Christians in Jerusalem had reached 5,000 men (Acts 4:4) in addition to their families. This was a significant number, and it made the Christians in Jerusalem almost equal in size to the Pharisees, whom the Jewish historian Josephus reports to have included about 6,000 men.[18]

Such dramatic growth brought the apostles into conflict with the authorities, and after they healed a lame man and preached the gospel in the temple, Peter and John were arrested by the Sanhedrin—the Jewish ruling council—and told not to teach in Jesus' name (Acts 3–4).

News of the miracles the apostles were performing reached neighboring towns, and people began bringing the sick and possessed to Jerusalem to be healed (Acts 5:16). They then returned home with the Christian faith, and Jesus' prophecy that the Faith would be preached throughout Judea began to be fulfilled.

Because the apostles continued to preach, they were re-arrested. The Sanhedrin told them, "We strictly charged you not to teach in this name, yet here you have filled Jerusalem with your teaching and you intend to bring this man's blood upon us" (Acts 5:28). The latter remark was a reference to the apostles' blaming the ruling council for Jesus' death—something that could stir up public opposition against them and possibly even violence. Consequently, this time the apostles were not simply released with a warning, and the council had them physically beaten (Acts 5:40).

At this point, the Jerusalem church was conducting a large-scale poverty relief program. Believers sold property they had and brought the proceeds to the apostles. The Christian community grew so large, however, that the program became unwieldy, and accusations were made that it wasn't being run fairly. Some Greek-speaking Jewish Christians argued that the widows of their group were being neglected in the daily food distribution (Acts 6:1). The apostles realized that sorting out conflicts like this would distract them from their teaching mission, so they appointed a group of seven reputable men to oversee the program on their behalf (Acts 6:2–4).

Each of these men appears to have been a Greek-speaking Jew, for they all have Greek names. One was St. Stephen, who became the Catholic Church's first martyr. Stephen himself worked miracles in Jesus' name, and it led him into a conflict with men from a local synagogue. He was taken before the Sanhedrin, and when he made a speech defending the Christian faith, the crowd became so enraged that they rushed him, drove him out of the city, and stoned him (Acts 6:8–7:60).

Stephen's martyrdom had several consequences for the Jerusalem church. It galvanized a young Pharisee named Saul into action. He approved of the stoning (Acts 7:58) and began leading a major persecution: "Saul was ravaging the church, and entering house after house, he dragged off men and women and committed them to prison" (Acts 8:3).

The persecution was so severe that the Jerusalem Christians "were all scattered throughout the region of Judea and Samaria, except the apostles" (Acts 8:1). Thus, God used the persecution to carry the Christian faith throughout these regions, again in accord with Jesus' prophecy, as "those who were scattered went about preaching the word" (Acts 8:4).

One was St. Philip the Evangelist (not the apostle of the same name). He, like Stephen, was one of the seven chosen to oversee the Jerusalem poverty relief effort. Luke recounts that, as a result of the persecution in Jerusalem, Philip went northward to a city in Samaria, where he performed miracles and converted many Samaritans (Acts 8:5–13). The apostles then came to the city and gave the sacrament of confirmation to the Samaritans, acknowledging their place in the Church (Acts 8:14–17). This represented a breaking of barriers, because even though the Samaritans worshipped the God of Israel and observed their own version of the Mosaic Law, they were traditionally excluded from the Jewish people and considered half-Gentile (see John 4:9).

Philip also broke another barrier. After leaving Samaria, he traveled south and met a eunuch who was court treasurer for the queen of the Ethiopians. He was a worshipper of God who had traveled to Jerusalem on pilgrimage, and he was now returning home. When Philip encountered him, the eunuch was reading aloud from Isaiah. This book was probably very dear to him. Eunuchs traditionally were excluded from God's people (Lev. 21:20; Deut. 23:1), but Isaiah prophesied that they would be acceptable to God, who would give the eunuchs who worshipped him an everlasting name (Isa. 56:3–5; cf. Wis. 3:14). The prophecy was fulfilled for this eunuch, whom Philip evangelized and then baptized, bringing him into the people of God, despite his traditionally excluded status (Acts 8:26–39).

While Philip was evangelizing, "Saul, still breathing threats and murder against the disciples of the Lord, went to the high priest and asked him for letters to the synagogues at Damascus, so that if he found any belonging to the way, men or women, he might bring them bound to Jerusalem" (Acts 9:1–2). But as he journeyed to Damascus, Jesus appeared to him and dramatically converted him (Acts. 9:3–19). He then began preaching Jesus in the synagogues of Damascus (Acts 9:20). When a persecution forced him to flee to Jerusalem, he was taken under the wing of St. Barnabas (Acts 9:23–28).

Despite Philip's preaching to Samaritans and the Ethiopian eunuch, the Faith hadn't yet spread to mainstream Gentiles. This happened when God directed St. Peter to preach to the Roman centurion Cornelius and his household. As he preached, the Holy Spirit fell upon the Gentiles, and they began speaking in tongues. This showed Peter that they were fully acceptable to God, and he baptized them (Acts 10:1–48). Some in the Jerusalem church objected, but Peter explained what happened, and they concluded, "Then to the Gentiles also God has granted repentance unto life" (Acts 11:18). Those who had been scattered by the persecution also began preaching the gospel to Gentiles in Antioch (in Syria), resulting in non-Jewish converts there (Acts 11:19–21).

Barnabas brought Paul to Antioch, and the two made it their missionary home base. It also was here that the followers of Jesus first became known as "Christians" (Acts 11:26).

Around this time, King Herod Agrippa—grandson of Herod the Great—martyred St. James, the son of Zebedee (Acts 12:1). He was the first of the Twelve apostles to suffer this fate. Herod also tried to kill Peter, but God miraculously freed him, and he left Jerusalem, beginning an international ministry that would take him to Rome (Acts 12:2–17; 1 Pet. 5:13).

The Holy Spirit also called Barnabas and Paul to an international mission, and from Antioch they began what is known as the First Missionary Journey. It took them to the island of Cyprus and to various regions in modern Turkey, before they returned to Antioch (Acts 13:1–14:28).

They arrived back in Antioch around A.D. 48, meaning fifteen years had passed since the Crucifixion in A.D. 33. All this time, the Christian faith had been taught exclusively by oral preaching—by Tradition—with no New Testament writings. But about this time, that started to change.

3

The Writing of the New Testament

LETTERS IN THE NEW TESTAMENT AGE

Before we discuss the individual books of the New Testament, let's talk about how writing in general worked in this period. It was not an easy process. The vast majority of people were illiterate and thus couldn't write. Most who could were able only to write simple things like their names or bills of sale.

This was true even among Jews. Sometimes the claim is made that all Jewish boys were taught to read the Torah, but the evidence doesn't support this. First-century literacy rates among Jews were comparable to those among Greeks and Romans. Jewish people obviously valued writing. The Torah was central to their religion. But the average person couldn't read it for himself and depended on it being read aloud in the synagogues (Luke 4:16; Acts 13:15, 27).

The fact that some *were* able to read it gave them added prestige. This is why "the scribes"—people able to read and write—were among the religious leaders Jesus had to contend with, and it's why they were set alongside religious leaders like the "chief priests" (Matt. 2:4; 16:21; 20:18) and the Pharisees (Matt. 5:20; 12:38; 15:1).

The Christian community had the same expectation that the average person would encounter the word of God orally rather than reading it for himself. Thus, at the end of 1 Thessalonians, Paul says, "I adjure you by the Lord that this letter be read to all the brethren" (1 Thess. 5:27). Similarly, he tells Timothy to "attend to the public reading of scripture" (1 Tim. 4:13). And the book of Revelation pronounces a blessing on the lectors who proclaim it: "Blessed is he who reads aloud the words of the prophecy" (Rev. 1:3).

When people in the ancient world wanted to write something more than just their signature or a bill of sale, it was usually a letter.[19] Ordinary people didn't compose lengthy treatises or books.

Like us, ancient people wanted to keep in touch with friends and loved ones, and before telephones and the internet, that meant letters. The ancients loved receiving letters—even if they couldn't read. They simply had a literate person read the letters to them.

Many ancient letters have pleas for the receiver to write back quickly and let the sender know how things are going. Sometimes they have rebukes for not responding sooner. We even have one letter in which a frustrated Egyptian says he is sending blank papyrus so the receiver won't have an excuse for not writing back promptly!

Most letters were just one page long, and they often said little more than the ancient equivalent of "I'm fine; how are you?" Yet people loved getting them. It was the only way they had to stay in touch.

DECIDING TO WRITE

If people wanted to *receive* letters, what caused a person to decide to *send* one? Sometimes it was to discuss an important event that had taken place.

That's why John wrote Revelation. On the island of Patmos, he received a major prophetic vision on a Sunday ("the Lord's day"; Rev. 1:10), so he sent a letter to the seven Asian churches to which the vision directed him to write (Rev. 1:11). Galatians was also prompted by an important event. Paul learned there was a heresy spreading in the Galatian churches, and he dashed off a letter to combat it (Gal. 1:1–7).

Normally, letters were sent for less dramatic reasons. A person might decide to write because he'd just received a letter and wanted to write back. This seems to be why Paul wrote 1 Corinthians as he refers to several matters the Corinthians had written him about (1 Cor. 7:1, 25; 8:1; 12:1; 16:1).

Sometimes, a person might write because a good scribe was available. This may have happened with Romans, which Paul wrote from Corinth. Paul had never visited Rome (Rom. 1:10–13) and was not planning on visiting immediately because he was going to Jerusalem next (Rom. 15:25–32). However, we know Romans was written by a scribe named Tertius, who greets the Romans without any introduction, suggesting they knew him (Rom. 16:22). It's likely that Tertius was a Roman Christian who visited Corinth. Paul then used the occasion to have Tertius write a letter to introduce himself.

Sometimes the fact that a person was going on a trip and could carry the letter was what prompted the decision to write. This may be the case with some of Paul's letters. Ephesians, Colossians, and Philemon were all sent to Asia at the same time using a courier named Tychicus, and it's likely

Paul sent some letters because Tychicus was already going to the region.

Sometimes there was more than one reason a person decided to write. Paul wrote to thank the Philippians for a donation they sent him during his imprisonment (Phil. 1:5; 4:18), but it's likely that they also sent him a letter with the donation. He was probably responding to both the donation and the letter that accompanied it.

PREPARING TO WRITE

The first step in preparing to write was finding a scribe. Even people who knew how to read usually didn't pen their own letters but rather employed a trained professional.

Rich people sometimes had slaves who were trained scribes, but ordinary people had to hire a scribe. Either way, it involved spending money. You had to pay either a slave's upkeep or a scribe's wages.

The scribe needed something to write on, and this was usually papyrus—an early form of paper made from reeds that grew along the banks of the Nile. Papyrus reeds were several inches thick, and once harvested they would be cut open and the pulpy inside was sliced into strips. These were pressed together to form a smooth writing surface. Papyrus was exported from Egypt and used all over the Roman world.

The other major writing material was parchment, which was made from animal skins (of calves, sheep, goats) that had been scraped smooth and stretched out to dry. Parchment was very durable and could be made anywhere (not just Egypt), but it seems to have been more expensive, and most people didn't use it for letters.

A scribe also needed ink and reed pens to write with, but these were inexpensive and easy to come by.

COMPOSING THE LETTER

When composing a letter, the sender would tell the scribe what he wanted written. Sometimes, he would simply give the scribe a general idea of what he wanted it to say, and the scribe would put it in his own words. This was common if the sender was illiterate and not skilled at composing good sentences.

Other times, particularly if the sender was a literary figure known for the quality of his letters—like the Roman author Cicero (106–43 B.C.)—he would dictate. If the scribe was trained in shorthand, he could keep up with dictation at normal, conversational speed. However, if the scribe didn't know shorthand (most did not), the author would dictate slowly, word by word.

Usually, the scribe served not just as a transcriptionist but as an editor, and he had some degree of input into how the letter was phrased. Scholars have noticed stylistic differences among the letters of Paul in the New Testament, and this suggests Paul used different scribes in the course of his career. Each scribe would make suggestions to Paul about how he might want to word things, and this would add a slightly different flavor to Paul's writings depending on which scribe he was using.

During dictation, the scribe usually took notes on reusable materials. He might write in ink on parchment or scratch notes on wooden frames coated with wax. The ink on the parchment could be washed off or the wax reconditioned so that the temporary writing surface could be used again.

Surprisingly, people in the first century didn't write at desks. Writing desks hadn't been invented, and, although they did have tables, they didn't use them for writing. Instead, the artistic and literary evidence shows scribes would sit and use a knee or a tunic stretched between their knees, to support the writing surface.

Writing also wasn't a solitary activity. By modern standards, the ancients lived in tiny, crowded dwellings, and they were seldom alone. They didn't value privacy the way we do, and other people were usually present when a letter was being dictated. We see evidence of this when Paul is emphasizing how few Corinthians he baptized and he suddenly remembers that he baptized the household of Stephanas (1 Cor. 1:16). We know that Stephanas had recently come to Paul (1 Cor. 16:17), so he probably was in the room and reminded Paul of the fact as he was dictating.

This means that pictures we see in later Christian art of Paul or one of the other biblical authors writing alone at a desk are based on the writing practices of their own day rather than those used in the first century. A more accurate picture would be of the biblical author dictating to a scribe who had writing materials on his lap, with other Christians in the background listening.

PREPARING TO SEND

After dictation, the scribe would depart and prepare a copy for the sender to review. If he wasn't satisfied, the sender could tell the scribe to make changes, and a new draft would be prepared. When he was satisfied—and if he himself was literate—he would sign the letter so it could be sent.

This didn't mean writing his name at the bottom the way we do today. It meant adding a personal note in his own hand. This note performed the same function as a modern signature—authenticating the letter using the penmanship of the sender—but it also incorporated the function of a modern postscript or "p.s." It let the sender add an additional short message he wanted to communicate, such as a final greeting or news of something that happened while the scribe was preparing the letter to be sent.

We see Paul doing this in his letters. We can often tell where his scribe's handwriting broke off and his own began, as when he told the Galatians, "See with what large letters I am writing to you with my own hand" (Gal. 6:11), or when he told the Thessalonians to pay attention to his penmanship so they could distinguish his letters from others: "I, Paul, write this greeting with my own hand. This is the mark in every letter of mine; it is the way I write" (2 Thess. 3:17; see also 2:2). This shows that—even though he was literate—Paul didn't write his letters himself, but used scribes.

Senders also put information in the postscript that they considered confidential and didn't want the scribe or others in the house to know about. The postscript was a good place for this because it wasn't dictated out loud and the letter would be sealed immediately afterward, preventing others from reading it.

Today we seal letters inside envelopes, but in the ancient world they were folded and then tied with a piece of cord—often a fiber pulled from the edge of the papyrus. A bit of clay was then used to seal the knot. This played the same function as our sealing an envelope—to secure the letter and keep anyone from reading it in transit. If the sender was from the upper class and had a signet—a personal seal—he would press it into the clay, adding extra proof the letter was from him.

SENDING THE LETTER

Once sealed, the letter was given to a carrier for delivery. There were no regular mailmen, and ordinary people didn't have access to the Roman military and diplomatic mail service.

If you were rich, you could have a slave—perhaps the scribe who wrote the letter—make the journey to deliver it, but if you were an ordinary person you had to make do with travelers who happened to be going where you needed a letter sent. This traveler-based system is still used today in parts of the developing world that don't have regular postal service.

Frequently, the fact someone was taking a trip would be what motivated a person to write. If you knew someone was heading to where your friend or relative lived, that would be a good time to write.

We know the couriers of many New Testament letters. Romans was carried by a woman named Phoebe (Rom. 16:1); Ephesians, Colossians, and Philemon were carried by a man named Tychicus (Eph. 6:21, Col. 4:7–9, Philem. 10–12); and 1 Peter was carried by Silvanus (Peter says he has written his audience "by Silvanus," which was a common way of introducing the letter carrier to the recipients; 1 Pet. 5:12).

RECEIVING A LETTER

When the letter arrived, it was common for the carrier to read it aloud, assuming the carrier was literate.

Often the carrier was present when the letter was being written, and he could provide extra details, clarify points that might be confusing, and imitate the sender's tone of voice to make sure the emotions came through properly. If the carrier was about to return where he came from—as with a slave dispatched to deliver a letter—it was common for the recipient to dictate a reply and send it back with him.

The letters of the New Testament are like other ancient letters in many ways, but they are also different in ways that would have surprised the recipients. One difference in Paul's letters is that he often names coauthors. First Corinthians is from Paul *and* Sosthenes; 2 Corinthians, Philippians, and Colossians are from Paul *and* Timothy; and 1 and 2 Thessalonians are from Paul *and* Silvanus *and* Timothy.

Today we rarely send letters jointly, and people in the ancient world were no different, so Paul's habit of listing coauthors is startling. He presumably did this to signal how much he valued the help of his coworkers and to signal the recipients that he wasn't writing just his own opinions; his associates also endorsed what he said. Thus, in Galatians he says he is writing together with "all the brethren who are with me" (Gal. 1:2). The implication is: *everybody* is in agreement with what I'm about to say, so take it seriously!

The size of the New Testament letters is even more startling. Ancient letters were an average of eighty-seven words long,[20] which is much shorter than *any* of the New Testament letters. Even a literary figure like Cicero wrote letters that averaged only 295 words. The only New Testament letters shorter than this are 2 John (245 words in Greek) and 3 John (219 words). Paul's *shortest* letter—Philemon (335 words)—is longer than Cicero's *average* one.

Imagine what the Romans must have thought when they got Paul's letter to them. At 7,111 words, Romans is *eighty-two times longer* than the average ancient letter! They must have been gobsmacked to receive such a lengthy letter from a man who had never even visited their church.

The Roman Christians also would have been impressed by something else: how much Paul's letter to them *cost*. Today, writing and sending a letter is a trivial expense, but it was far from trivial in the first century. Papyrus had to be made by hand and was expensive. So was hiring a scribe. This is one reason ancient letters were short.

Cross-cultural cost comparisons are always tricky, but Randolph Richards did a helpful study of how much Paul's letters would have cost, and he estimates that Romans would have cost Paul around $2,275 to produce (in 2004 dollars).[21] This would have paid for the prepublication drafts of the letter as well as one copy to send to Rome and one to keep for his records, which was the common practice among authors of literary letters. Even if we ignore the prepublication costs of preparing drafts, a single, finished copy of Romans would have cost the equivalent of $868!

The fact that the New Testament letters are so much longer than what ordinary people sent—and that so much money was spent on them—illustrates how the biblical authors considered them important works of literature and not simply personal missives.

BOOKS IN THE NEW TESTAMENT AGE

Most people in the ancient world didn't write anything longer than short letters, but some wrote entire books. Then as now, writing a book that other people would want to read involved more literary skill than composing a letter. Books had to appeal to a broader audience made up of people who weren't friends or relatives, and authors had to sustain their attention for a much longer period.

Consequently, the number of people who could write books in a largely illiterate society was quite small. To acquire the skills needed to write one, a person needed to read a great deal—to learn the skills other authors were using—and to practice by writing shorter works and building the literary muscle needed to pull off something as long as a book.

These aspects of the book-writing process are the same in our day, but other aspects are different. For example, some ancient authors—particularly in the Jewish world—didn't sign their works. Thus, the historical books of the Old Testament don't bear the names of their authors. They weren't seeking personal fame the way Greek and Roman literary authors were. What was important to them was that they were communicating the history of God's people.

This is likely why the four evangelists didn't identify themselves by name in the Gospels and Acts. Since they were writing histories of Jesus and the early Church, they followed the practice of the Old Testament historians. What was important for them was communicating what God had done through Jesus and what he was doing with his new Christian people. They weren't trying to build their own reputations.

That didn't mean the early Church was unaware of who these men were. As Luke's prefaces to his Gospel and Acts reveal (Luke 1:1–4; Acts 1:1–2), he was writing to a man called Theophilus, who certainly knew who Luke was. Theophilus was likely Luke's patron who paid for the cost of producing the Gospel and Acts. However, Luke was just a servant of Christ and didn't feel the need to immortalize himself by citing his name in the text.

Another difference is that there was no such thing as copyright law. Today, copyrights protect the intellectual property of authors and publishers. This allows them to make money from their efforts, which encourages them to produce more books and enrich society. This is a key reason we have so many more books available to us today.

But there were no copyrights in the ancient world. As a result, if you had access to a book and you wanted a copy of it, you simply had a scribe make one for you. The only person who made money on that transaction was the scribe (if he wasn't a slave). The original author didn't make a denarius, so he had to have other motives for writing, such as achieving literary fame or spreading God's word. He also had to have some other source of income as it was impossible to earn a living as an author.

SOURCE MATERIAL FOR BOOKS

The fact there were no copyrights meant authors were legally free to copy from and use another writer's works when composing their own.

Of course, if you copied something from a famous literary author—like Cicero or Sophocles—and tried to pass it off as your own, people would look down on that. But for people who were just interested in getting out the truth, it was different. Their egos weren't involved, and—on the principle that all truth is God's truth—they would use material from earlier sources and tailor their presentation to help serve the needs of their audience.

For one anonymous historian to use material from another anonymous historian didn't step on anyone's reputation. Thus, in the Old Testament, we see the author of 1–2 Chronicles using and condensing material from the books of 1–2 Samuel and 1–2 Kings to produce a shorter history of God's people. Similarly, in the New Testament we see Matthew and Luke using material from Mark, which they supplement to provide fuller accounts of Jesus' ministry.

The ancients sometimes drew a distinction between two kinds of works. The first was an unpolished collection of material that didn't have literary pretentions and was meant to serve basic information needs. In Greek, these works were called collections of *hypomnêmata*, and in Latin they were called *comentarii*. Both of these terms meant, roughly, "notes," "memoranda," or "things to be remembered."

Sometimes authors would publish books of this nature as reference works or textbooks as the physician Galen did with some of his medical texts. Other times they would be published in this form for reasons of expediency and timeliness. Thus, Julius Caesar published his *Gallic Wars* in the form of *commentarii*.

Authors might prepare works like this as a prelude to more polished literary productions on the same subject. Sometimes one author would prepare *hympomnêmata* for use by *another* author. He might even sell it to the second author as the basis for the latter's literary work. This is similar to how major authors today may use research assistants to prepare the material on which they will base their novels or nonfiction works.

When the time came to produce the literary work, an author would take the initial, unpolished one, put the material in proper literary order, supplement or trim it, and polish its style before publishing it as a new work. As we will see, this may explain some of the differences between Mark's Gospel and those of Matthew and Luke.[22]

PUBLISHING THE BOOK

As they were writing a book, ancient authors often would read it or parts of it out loud for purposes of getting feedback. They might read it to their friends or in public lectures. This is similar to how modern authors like C.S. Lewis, J.R.R. Tolkien, and other members of their "Inklings" literary group would read and discuss stories they were working on.

Ancient authors also might loan copies of works they were preparing to friends, which sometimes resulted in them being accidentally published early, since if a friend took a liking to a book, all he had to do was have a scribe make a copy of it for his own uses.

Most of the time, however, books would be released only when the author felt they were ready for publication. The author would have a scribe or a team of scribes make copies for distribution, some of which might be put on sale.

That meant the author typically bore the costs of publication, which included both writing materials and scribal labor on the prepublication drafts as well as copies of the final, published edition. These costs were substantial. Based on the estimates Randolph Richards proposed for the costs of Paul's letters, we can estimate that a copy of each the four Gospels would have cost the following:[23]

Matthew: $2,238
Mark: $1,379
Luke: $2,377
John: $1,909

Those are just the costs for a *single* copy of the final edition. They don't account for the cost of producing the drafts that led up to the final edition or the multiple copies that the author would have produced at the publication stage, and there would have been several of these. Whereas an author might be satisfied with producing two copies of a letter—one to send and one to keep for his records—books like the Gospels, Acts, and Revelation would have been launched with multiple copies issued simultaneously.

For example, Revelation was sent to seven churches (Rev. 1:4). John also would have kept a copy for himself, which means launching the book involved at least eight copies. Revelation is about 39 percent longer than Romans, which means that a single copy would have cost around $1,203. Launching the book with eight copies would have cost $9,624—and that's ignoring the prepublication costs of preparing and revising drafts.

For a long time, it was assumed that when the Gospels were published, only a single copy was given to a single church that was its intended audience. However, more recent research has indicated that the Gospels were meant for broad audiences—not just a lone church somewhere.[24] This suggests that, as with the book of Revelation, the publication of the Gospels would have involved multiple copies. No wonder Luke needed the patron Theophilus to underwrite the costs of producing his Gospel and Acts!

The expenses involved in producing books meant that only rich people could afford to write them. It also meant rich people were the only ones who could afford to buy them, though an institution like a church could pool resources and pay for copies that few, if any, of its individual members could afford.

This is why the Roman authorities went after Christian scriptures in the age of persecutions. If they could strip a church of its holy books, they could deprive its members of crucial resources that couldn't easily be replaced.

It's also why Christians viewed turning over the scriptures to the authorities as such an act of betrayal. Today you could replace a whole Bible for just a few dollars, but then a complete copy of the scriptures was a precious and virtually irreplaceable collection. Those who did hand over the scriptures (Latin, *tradere*, "to hand over") became known as *traditores*, from which we get the English word *traitors*.

BOOKS AS PHYSICAL OBJECTS

The high cost of books also meant authors had to keep them short. That's why the individual "books" of the Bible seem brief compared to modern books.

Today, a typical novel is between 70,000 and 120,000 words long. By comparison, Luke, the longest of the Gospels and the longest book of the New Testament, is fewer than 20,000 words.

There was a second reason why ancient books were short: they were bound differently than modern ones. Today, when we think of a book, we think of a specific kind called a *codex*. In a codex, the pages are joined together at the book's spine, and we can flip to whatever page we want. However, in the ancient world, people almost never published books in this form. They did have codices, but they were small and were used like notepads—a place to jot down small bits of text.

Codices and scrolls

Instead, the ancients published books in the form of scrolls, where an individual page is joined to other pages on both the right and the left. This meant that instead of flipping from one page to another, you rolled or unrolled the scroll to get to the point you wanted. This also kept books short. A modern Bible is thousands of pages long, and nobody would want to roll through a scroll containing thousands of pages! Indeed, if you were in the middle of such a scroll, the weight of the two ends would be so great that the pages would tear and the scroll would come apart.

If someone wanted to write at length about a subject, he had to use multiple scrolls—that is, publish multiple books. That's why, if you read some ancient works, you'll see them divided into "books." Josephus's account of the Great Jewish

Revolt—found in his work *The Jewish War*—is divided into seven books. That's because it originally was published as seven scrolls. Similarly, his history of ancient Israel, *Antiquities of the Jews*, is in twenty books because it was published as a collection of twenty scrolls.

The costs of complete copies of such lengthy works were daunting enough that it created a market for more affordable, abridged versions. These were the ancient equivalent of *Reader's Digest* "condensed" books, and they were known as *epitomes*. An epitome let you get the basic message of a longer work—all its key points—without the expense and the time involved in acquiring and reading the whole thing.

Epitomes were popular in the ancient world, and we even find them in the Bible. The book of Chronicles (originally a single book, though it's now printed as two) is an epitome of the history found in the books of Samuel and Kings. Similarly, most of 2 Maccabees is an epitome that abridges a five-volume history by Jason of Cyrene (2 Macc. 2:23).

Except for Psalms, which was designed to fill five scrolls, the books of the Bible were designed to fit into single scrolls. That's why the Gospels are the length they are. Sometimes short works were bound together in a single scroll—such as the minor prophets being published as *The Twelve* or having the catholic epistles together in one scroll—but you could never bind the entire New Testament in a scroll, much less the Old Testament.

How did the transition to the modern form of book—the codex—happen? This was an innovation of the Christian movement. Scholars aren't sure why, but the early Christians began showing a clear preference for the codex. The reasons are mysterious. Both forms of book had advantages and disadvantages, and as long as books were short, neither the scroll nor the codex had a decisive advantage.

Nevertheless, Christians decided to reject centuries of literary tradition and start binding their sacred books in a form that was previously associated with informal note-taking. The most likely explanation is that there was an influential, early edition of a key work—maybe a Gospel or a collection of Paul's letters—that appeared as a codex and got Christians thinking of this as a suitable form for holy books. It then became a mark of Christian identity to use codices rather than scrolls.

THE FOUR GOSPELS

The most important documents of the New Testament are the four Gospels. They tell us the story of Jesus, who is at the core of the Christian faith. So, what can we say about how they were written?

A starting point is the names we refer to them by: Matthew, Mark, Luke, and John. You sometimes hear people say the Gospels were anonymous and these names weren't added until later, sometime in the second century, but this doesn't fit the evidence.

It's true that—following the practice of the Old Testament historical authors—the evangelists don't name themselves, but they didn't write anonymously, and they were certainly known to their original audiences. Luke's patron Theophilus knew who he was. John expressly identifies its author as the beloved disciple, whose name was known to the intended audience (John 21:20–24). Similarly, the authors of Matthew and Mark were known to their audiences.

The idea that the names were added to the Gospels late is also problematic. If the Gospels had circulated for an extended period with no names, people would have begun calling them by a variety of names.

The Gospel of Matthew, for example, might have been called not only "the Gospel according to Matthew" but also things like "the Gospel according to James," "the Gospel of the Jews," or "the Life of Jesus Christ." We would have a record of this early confusion if it occurred, and we don't. Matthew's Gospel—like each of the four—is known by only *one* name in early Christian literature, showing that it had this name very early.

There was a need for the names as soon as more than one Gospel was in existence. The first Christians needed a way to distinguish one Gospel from another, and the way they picked was to identify them by the author. Since the Gospels were written in the first century, the need to distinguish them existed then, and thus they began circulating with their current names in the first century.[25] This means they came to be known by these names within living memory of the time they were written, when people were aware of who the authors were, and therefore we need to take the authors' names seriously.

In fact, the names themselves provide evidence they are authentic. While ancient writers sometimes attributed their works to long-dead authors to increase the prestige of their works, that wouldn't have applied to the Gospels. Matthew, Mark, and Luke weren't the people you'd pick to add prestige. Their names may be famous *today*, but that's because of their Gospels. At the time, things were different.

Mark and Luke weren't even apostles, but junior associates. Mark was initially a companion of Barnabas and Paul and later served as Peter's interpreter. Luke was just one of Paul's many traveling companions. Both are mentioned only a handful of times in the New Testament, and the mentions aren't all good. Mark abandoned his first mission trip (Acts 13:13), and Paul refused to take him on a second mission.

This led to such a sharp argument between him and Barnabas that the two dissolved their partnership (Acts 15:37–40). Mark eventually redeemed himself (2 Tim. 4:11), but his early failure remained a black mark.

Luke's reputation was unblemished, but he is named only three times (Col. 4:14; 2 Tim. 4:11; Philem. 24), making him far less prominent than other Pauline companions such as Timothy (twenty-five mentions), Titus (thirteen mentions), and Silas (twelve mentions).

Matthew's Gospel is the most Jewish, which makes Matthew the last person whose name would give it prestige. Not only was Matthew only a mid-level apostle (note his placement when the names of the Twelve are given; see Matt. 10:2–4; Mark 3:16–19; Luke 6:14–16; Acts 1:13), he was also a tax collector (Matt. 9:9), and tax collectors were hated by Jews, who saw them as collaborators with the Romans and as sinners (Matt. 9:11; 18:17).

The only major name attached to a Gospel is John, and while John, son of Zebedee, was prominent (note his placement in the lists of the Twelve), there is a question whether the fourth Gospel was written by him or another lesser-known eyewitness named John.[26] Thus, with the possible exception of John, the evangelists' names aren't those one would pick to lend authority to the Gospels.

We thus have good evidence that two of the Gospels—Matthew and John—were written by eyewitnesses, and the other two—Mark and Luke—were written by close associates of apostles.

THE ORDER OF THE GOSPELS

In what order were the Gospels written? We're familiar with their canonical order, which places Matthew first, Mark second, and so on, but this doesn't mean that they were composed in that order.

It's clear there is a relationship of some kind between three of the Gospels—Matthew, Mark, and Luke. They tell the story of Jesus in a similar way, so they are referred to as the *synoptic* Gospels since they give us a common picture of his ministry (Greek, *sun* "together" + *opsis* "seeing"). The study of how they are related is known in biblical scholarship as *the Synoptic Problem*, and it can shed light on the order in which they were written.

The relationship between the synoptic Gospels is so close that many passages in them record events from Jesus' ministry in exactly the same words. This applies not only to quotations from Jesus but also to the words of the narrative describing what he did. This suggests that after the first evangelist wrote his Gospel, two of the other evangelists included material from his Gospel in their own.

For much of Church history, it was common to hold that Matthew was the first to write. This is likely because Matthew's is the Gospel most clearly written for a Jewish audience (i.e., Jewish Christians). Since the first believers were Jews, it would be natural to assume that the most Jewish Gospel was written first.

But in recent years, most scholars have become convinced that Mark was first. There are several reasons. One is Mark's style, which is less polished. This makes it seem like Mark wrote first and then Matthew and Luke polished the language when they wrote.

Furthermore, Mark omits material one would normally expect in a biography such as information about Jesus' birth and family lineage. Also, the original edition of Mark may not have included the appearances of Jesus to the disciples after his resurrection. The current ending of Mark, which contains these appearances (see Mark 16:9–20), is not to be found in the earliest manuscripts of Mark.

Scholars have wondered why he would leave these out. Did something stop him from finishing his Gospel? Was it accidentally published before he was ready? There have been many proposals. A recent one is that Mark never intended to produce a finished literary work. Instead, he was making an unpolished collection of notes on Jesus' ministry—what the ancients called *hypomnêmata*—and he left it to others to arrange, supplement, and polish the material.[27]

This fits with some very early testimony we have about Mark. In the early second century, a bishop named Papias wrote a five-volume work on Jesus, and he quoted an earlier, first-century figure known as John the Elder. According to Papias:

> This also the elder said: "Mark, having become the interpreter of Peter, wrote down accurately, though not in order, whatsoever he remembered of the things said or done by Christ. For he neither heard the Lord nor followed him, but afterward, as I said, he followed Peter, who gave his teaching in the form of anecdotes, but with no intention of giving a connected account of the Lord's discourses, so that Mark committed no error while he thus wrote some things as he remembered them. For he was careful of one thing, not to omit any of the things which he had heard, and not to state any of them falsely."[28]

Papias says John the Elder was an eyewitness of Jesus' ministry and was in a good position to know the authors of the New Testament. According to him, Mark was concerned to accurately preserve the facts about Jesus but without putting them in polished literary order. That task was done by the later evangelists.

John the Elder's statement that Mark was based on Peter's preaching also suggests it was the first Gospel written, as it was based on an oral source—Peter—rather than a prior written work.

Matthew and Luke then appear to have supplemented Mark's material with information one would ordinarily expect in a biography such as the circumstances surrounding Jesus' birth and family background. They wrote what are called the *Infancy Narratives* dealing with Jesus' early life (Matt. 1:18–2:23; Luke 1:5–2:52) and provided genealogies to reveal his family background and link to King David (Matt. 1:1–17; Luke 3:23–38). At the end of their Gospels, they also include information about his appearances after the Resurrection (Matt. 28:9–20; Luke 24:13–53). And in general, they flesh out the story of Jesus' ministry by recording more of his teachings and the events that happened to him.

Where did they get this material? The most common opinion today is that for at least part of it, they relied on a source called Q (from the German, *Quelle*, "source"). Scholars have suggested this source to explain more than 200 verses in Matthew that are very similar to verses in Luke.

However, not everyone is convinced that there was a Q document. It could be that Mark wrote first, Matthew supplemented Mark, and then Luke drew the material otherwise attributed to Q from Matthew. Or it could be that Mark wrote first, Luke supplemented Mark, and then Matthew drew the "Q material" from Luke.

What is generally agreed is that John wrote last. John seems to expect his readers to already know about the synoptic Gospels. Early on, he is discussing John the Baptist, and he suddenly says, "John had not yet been put in prison" (John 3:24). You wouldn't know about John the Baptist being put in prison from anything else John says in his Gospel; it is a story recorded in the synoptics. It thus appears that John was written later and that he knew and expected his readers to know one or more of the synoptic Gospels.[29] This helps explain why John's Gospel is different from the others. He isn't interested in simply repeating what the synoptics said: he's interested in filling in some of the things they didn't have space to include.

THE DATES OF THE GOSPELS

Many scholars hold that the Gospels were written late in the first century with Mark being written between A.D. 60 and 75, Matthew being written around 80 to 90, Luke being written around 85, and John being written in the A.D. 90s. However, a careful look at the evidence suggests that these dates are too late.

Luke and Acts were written as a two-volume set: Acts picks up exactly where Luke leaves off (Luke 24:44–52; Acts 1:1–2), both are dedicated to the same man, Theophilus (Luke 1:1–4; Acts 1:1), and Acts refers to Luke as "the first book" (Acts 1:1), implying Acts is the second.

As we will see, there are good reasons to think Acts was written around the year 60 after Paul had been under house arrest in Rome for two years (Acts 28:30). It's very likely Luke and Acts were written in this period. Since it would take some time for each book to be composed, we can propose that Acts was written around A.D. 60 and Luke's Gospel was written just before that, around A.D. 59.

This would mean Mark was written earlier, for it was one of Luke's sources. John the Elder tells us Mark is based on the preaching he heard while he was Peter's interpreter, but that didn't happen until after he had been the traveling companion of Barnabas and Paul. After the Jerusalem Council of A.D. 49, Barnabas took Mark on a missionary journey to the island of Cyprus (Acts 15:39). This means Mark didn't become Peter's companion until A.D. 50 at the earliest, and we can thereby date Mark's Gospel to sometime in the 50s—say, around A.D. 55.

What about Matthew's Gospel? A number of passages in Matthew envision the Jerusalem temple still functioning, with Jewish Christians still attending it (Matt. 5:23–24;12:5; 23:20–21). This suggests Matthew was written before the temple was destroyed in A.D. 70.

A noteworthy passage is where Jesus tells Peter to pay the temple tax rather than giving offense to non-Christian Jews (Matt. 17:24–27). It's difficult to imagine Matthew writing this passage the way he did after A.D. 70 because after this date the Romans required Jews to pay the tax *not* to their own temple but to support the temple of Jupiter Best and Greatest in Rome.[30] If Matthew was writing after A.D. 70, to portray Jesus condoning the payment of this tax would have risked confusing, alienating, and outraging members of his audience. Jesus could even be understood as financially supporting idolatry so as "not to give offense"!

That suggests Matthew wrote after Mark but before the destruction of the temple, sometime between A.D. 55 and 70. If he took the "Q material" from Luke, it would place Matthew sometime in the A.D. 60s. This date is supported by the second-century Church Father St. Irenaeus of Lyons, who says Matthew wrote his Gospel "while Peter and Paul were preaching at Rome."[31] That is most naturally understood as a reference to the 60s when both Peter and

Paul were in Rome, though before their martyrdoms (likely 66 in the case of Peter and 67 in the case of Paul). Therefore, Matthew might have written around A.D. 63.

The dates proposed here are supported by the fact that each of the synoptics records Jesus predicting the destruction of the temple (Matt. 24:1–2; Mark 13:1–2; Luke 21:5–7) but none records the prophecy being fulfilled. They do record the fulfillment of other prophecies Jesus made—such as his own death and resurrection—since they were writing after these occurred. If they had been writing after A.D. 70, we would expect them to record the fulfillment of the temple prophecy, further showing Jesus to be a true prophet. But they don't. They depict it as a prophecy still to be fulfilled, with Christians needing to watch for it, flee from it when it happens, and pray that the fulfillment not take place when travel is difficult (Matt. 24:15–20; Mark 13:14–18; Luke 21:20–21).

This leaves us with the Gospel of John. It may have been written after the others, but that doesn't mean it was written late. There is a startling clue in the Greek that suggests it wasn't.

The Gospel's final chapter records Jesus making a prophecy about how Peter would die. Then, in many translations, the evangelist says, "This he said to show by what death he was to glorify God" (John 21:19). The translation uses the past tense—the death by which Peter *was* to glorify God—suggesting John was writing afterward.

But the Greek doesn't use the past tense. It uses the future tense: "by what death he *will glorify* [*doksasei*] God." It appears translators have so long assumed that John's Gospel was late that they've missed the fact the text indicates it was written *before* Peter's death around A.D. 66. That would allow us to propose a date around A.D. 65 for the Gospel of John.

THE BOOK OF ACTS

The end of Luke's Gospel sets up the beginning of Acts, so scholars have generally thought they were written around the same time. Those who hold Luke was written in the 70s or 80s think Acts was written then also. But we've suggested the two were written earlier.

This is because of how Acts is structured. It ends with St. Paul awaiting trial in Rome, and Paul's journey to Rome is a major theme in the book, set up as early as Acts 9:15–16. The theme becomes explicit when Paul announces he must see Rome after visiting Jerusalem (Acts 18:21). He then insists on going to Jerusalem, knowing he will be arrested (Acts 20:22–23; 21:10–14). When that occurs (Acts 21:33), the story of his journey to Rome takes over the narrative and dominates the last seven chapters of the book—one fourth of its twenty-eight chapters.

Yet, it ends inconclusively with Paul spending two years under house arrest and no word of what happened at his trial. Given the amount of drama building up to the trial, this would make no sense if the result of the trial were known. If Paul had been condemned, Luke would have the story of his glorious martyrdom or innocent suffering on account of Christ. If he had been acquitted, Luke would have recorded his glorious vindication. Other sources indicate that on this occasion he was released.[32] So why doesn't Luke record either his suffering or his vindication?

The logical explanation is that the trial simply hadn't yet happened. This is the only sensible explanation for why Acts cuts off suddenly after building to this moment for chapter after chapter. That tells us when Acts was published: two years after Paul's Roman imprisonment began. Many scholars think Paul's imprisonment began around A.D. 60, giving us a date of 62 for Acts. A stronger case, though, is that it began in 58, giving us a date of 60 for Acts.[33]

ST. PAUL'S LETTERS

It's often said that the first books of the New Testament were St. Paul's letters and the Gospels were written later. But we've seen that the Gospels were likely written in the A.D. 50s and 60s, which is the same time frame as Paul's letters. So how do they fit together?

We're fortunate to have Acts because it records Paul's travels up to A.D. 60 in great detail, allowing us to match his letters against the information in Acts and giving us a good idea of their dates.

1–2 Thessalonians

The first letter Paul wrote, at least among those in New Testament, was likely 1 Thessalonians. He founded the church of Thessalonica during his Second Missionary Journey (Acts 15:40–18:22), but he was able to stay for only three weeks before being driven away by persecution (Acts 17:1–10).

Consequently, he worried whether his new converts would remain true to the Faith, and from Athens he dispatched Timothy to visit them (1 Thess. 3:1–2; cf. Acts 17:15–34). Timothy rejoined Paul while he was staying in Corinth (Acts 18:5), and Paul was overjoyed to learn that the Thessalonian Christians were still faithful, leading to his first letter to them. First Thessalonians was written early in the Corinthian visit Luke records in Acts 18:1–18, which would point to the spring of A.D. 50.

Unfortunately, not everything went well in Thessalonica, and the Christians there picked up false ideas about the end of the world. They may have obtained these by misunderstanding what Paul wrote in 1 Thessalonians. Thus, he wrote them again a few weeks or months later, producing 2 Thessalonians.

Galatians

Another of Paul's early letters is to the churches of Galatia. This is a region in modern Turkey that he evangelized on his Second Missionary Journey. The Council of Jerusalem had already ruled that Gentile Christians didn't need to be circumcised (Acts 15:1–31; Gal. 2:1–10), so Paul was alarmed when he learned some people were telling his Gentile converts in Galatia they needed to become Jews to be saved. He wrote the letter to the Galatians in a white-hot fury, saying this was emphatically not the case. Based on internal clues, it is likely Paul wrote Galatians either around A.D. 50 when he was staying in Corinth (see Acts 18:11), or around A.D. 53 when he was staying in Ephesus (see Acts 19:8–10).

1-2 Corinthians

Paul maintained a substantial correspondence with the church he founded in the Greek city of Corinth, and two of these letters are in the New Testament.

Despite its name, 1 Corinthians isn't the first letter he wrote them. In 1 Corinthians 5:9, Paul refers to an earlier, lost letter. The Corinthians also wrote a lost letter to Paul in which they asked him several questions. Responding to these is one of the key things he does in 1 Corinthians (see 7:1, 25; 8:1; 12:1; 16:1, 12). Internal clues indicate Paul wrote this letter while he was staying in Ephesus (Acts 19:1–20:1), likely in late A.D. 53. At this point, Paul was conducting his Third Missionary Journey (Acts 18:23–21:17), which ran from A.D. 51 to 55.

Things didn't go well in Corinth, and rather than coming to them and making "another painful visit," Paul wrote a now-lost letter "with many tears" in which he took them to task (see 2 Cor. 2:1–4). Scholars refer to this as "the sorrowful letter" or "the severe letter." It was likely sent in early 54.

Paul then traveled to Macedonia (Acts 20:1–2), and it was here that he wrote 2 Corinthians in late 54 or early 55. The letter starts positively as news had reached Paul that the Corinthians had repented (2 Cor. 7:6–13). Unfortunately, it appears news arrived just as Paul was about to send the letter that some in Corinth were challenging his authority, and the mood of the letter changes dramatically. In the last three chapters (2 Cor. 10–13), he mounts a heated defense of his ministry as an apostle.

Fortunately, this defense seems to have worked, and Paul visited Corinth when he later traveled to Greece (Acts 20:2–3; see also Rom. 16:1–2).

Romans

While in Corinth in the spring of A.D. 55, Paul encountered a scribe named Tertius who apparently was from Rome (Rom. 16:22). Although Paul had been an apostle for many years, he had never visited the empire's capital, and he took the occasion of meeting Tertius to write a letter to the Roman Christians saying he hoped to visit soon.

His plan was to go to Jerusalem to deliver a collection he'd been taking up for the saints there and then come to Rome on what would have been the Fourth Missionary Journey (Rom. 16:25–26, 31).

It appears that Paul learned—from Tertius or someone else—that there were Christians in Rome who believed Gentiles must be circumcised, and he spends a great deal of the letter explaining the proper relationship between Jewish and Gentile Christians.

Ephesians, Philippians, Colossians, and Philemon

Unfortunately, the Fourth Missionary Journey didn't happen—at least not the way Paul expected. When he took the collection to Jerusalem, he was arrested (Acts 21:33) and spent the next several years in custody (Acts 24:27). Eventually, he used his right as a Roman citizen to have his case heard by the emperor Nero, and he was duly sent to Rome (Acts 25:11–12). He arrived there, by my estimate, in early A.D. 58 and then spent the next two years under house arrest awaiting trial (Acts 28:30).

Paul wrote several letters while in captivity. These are known as his *prison epistles.* Scholars debate exactly when they were composed, but they appear to have been written during his first Roman imprisonment between A.D. 58 and 60.

Several—Ephesians, Colossians, and Philemon—seem to have been sent at one time. The letter carrier of Ephesians and Colossians was Tychicus (Eph. 6:21–22; Col. 4:7–8), and he was accompanied by a slave named Onesimus (Philem. 10) who was going back to his master, Philemon, who was himself a Colossian (Col. 4:9).

There is a mystery connected with Ephesians. Paul knew that church well. He visited it several times and spent three years there (Acts 20:31). But Ephesians reads like Paul is writing people he's never met, and the letter has no personal greetings. Furthermore, the letter is addressed differently depending on which manuscript you examine. In some, it is addressed "To the saints who are in Ephesus also faithful in Christ Jesus." But in some manuscripts the phrase "in Ephesus" is missing.

Many scholars have proposed that what we think of as Ephesians is actually a circular letter sent to many churches in the area. Since Paul hadn't visited all of these, the letter lacks the expected tone and personal greetings. It may be that one copy was delivered to Ephesus, resulting in the words "in Ephesus" being in some manuscripts. And there is evidence copies also were sent elsewhere. It appears a copy of what is likely the same letter was sent to Laodicea (Col. 4:16).

Many themes in Ephesians are also found in Colossians, which isn't surprising since they were written to churches in the same area at the same time. It appears Paul hadn't visited Colossae (Col. 2:1), though he did know some Colossian Christians, perhaps having met them in other cities.

These included a man named Philemon, who hosted a church in his house (Philem. 1–2). When Paul dispatched Ephesians and Colossians with Tychicus, he also sent a personal letter to Philemon. It is very brief and deals with the situation of a runaway slave named Onesimus, whom Philemon owned. The apostle explains that after Onisemus fled, he met Paul and was converted to the Faith. Now he is a brother in Christ, and the apostle urges Philemon to receive him as a brother.

The final letter from this period is Philippians. Paul founded a church in Philippi during the Second Missionary Journey (Acts 16:12–40), and it sent him financial support more than once. They had underwritten his early evangelizing efforts in Thessalonica (Phil. 4:15–16), and they helped him again during his Roman imprisonment (Phil. 4:18). Paul thus writes to thank them, to update them on his situation, and to exhort them to live Christian lives.

1 Timothy and Titus

Early sources indicate that Paul was vindicated and released at his first trial in Rome[34] before later being re-arrested and martyred around A.D. 67.[35]

It appears that in the interim, Paul was able to fulfill his desire to evangelize in Spain in the far West of Europe (Rom. 15:24, 28; *1 Clement* 5:7). He also conducted ministry in the East, and during this time he wrote two letters to his protégés, Timothy and Titus. Because they served as pastors, these are known as *pastoral epistles.*

Likely written around A.D. 65, the letters instruct Paul's protégés on a variety of matters, including appointing and disciplining presbyters and deacons in the churches where they were ministering: Ephesus in the case of Timothy, and the island of Crete in the case of Titus. The fact that Paul entrusts them with such important tasks of church governance indicates how the two young men had matured as leaders and how apostles like Paul were transitioning important functions to the next generation of leaders.

2 Timothy

Paul's final letter is 2 Timothy. It is a pastoral epistle and a prison epistle because Paul had been taken into custody again. This time, he realizes that the attitude of the Roman authorities has changed and he will not be set free. He despairs of life, saying:

I am already on the point of being sacrificed; the time of my departure has come. I have fought the good fight, I have finished the race, I have kept the faith. Henceforth there is laid up for me the crown of righteousness, which the Lord, the righteous judge, will award to me on that day (2 Tim. 4:6–8).

The likely reason for the change in the Roman authorities' attitude is that after the Great Fire of Rome in A.D. 64,

Nero began using Christians as scapegoats, claiming they were arsonists.[36]

According to Pope St. Clement I, writing just a few years later, Paul was put to death "under the prefects."[37] This is most likely a reference to the prefects Nero left in charge while he was on an extended tour of Greece in the latter part of his reign.

Still, at the time the letter was written, Paul did not foresee his end arriving immediately, and he urges Timothy to come before the travel season closed in winter (2 Tim. 4:21). This suggests that the letter was written in the summer or fall of A.D. 66.

THE LETTER TO THE HEBREWS

Historically, the letter to the Hebrews was grouped with the epistles of St. Paul, but there were early doubts about whether it was written by him. This is why it's printed in Bibles just after the letters by Paul.

The early Church Fathers weren't confident that Paul wrote it. Pope St. Zephyrinus (r. 199–217) denied that it was by Paul.[38] Around A.D. 200, Tertullian said it was written by Barnabas,[39] and shortly afterward Origen mentioned traditions that it was written by Luke or Pope St. Clement I, though he concluded that "who wrote the epistle, in truth, God knows."[40]

Modern scholars generally have concluded that the letter wasn't written by Paul. It doesn't claim to be by him and lacks the usual marks of his letters. It likely was written by someone in his circle, however, and it mentions that his companion Timothy has just been released from prison (Heb. 13:23). We don't know any periods in Paul's life when Timothy was in prison, and the fact the letter doesn't mention Paul suggests it was written at least some time after his death when his martyrdom would no longer be news.

But the letter couldn't have been written too long after Paul's death, for it refers to the Jerusalem temple as still in operation, with the priests still offering sacrifices there (Heb. 8:4). The author certainly would have mentioned the temple's destruction in August of 70 if it had happened because it would have clinched his major line of argument, which was that the revelation of Christ has surpassed the Old Covenant and its worship that was "ready to vanish away" (Heb. 8:13).

Despite its connection with Italy (Heb. 13:24), the letter to the Hebrews doesn't refer to the disastrous "year of four emperors" that occurred in A.D. 69. This points to A.D. 68 as a likely date for its composition, which would fit with the progress of the Great Jewish Revolt that began in 66. By 68, a Jewish Christian could reasonably foresee that the time of the temple's destruction was drawing near, in keeping with Jesus' prophecy (Mark 13:1–2, 30).

THE CATHOLIC EPISTLES

Toward the end of the New Testament is a collection of seven letters that aren't associated with St. Paul. They are referred to as the *catholic epistles* (Greek, *katholikê*, "general," "universal") because most are written to broad audiences rather than to individual churches (though 2 John was written to a church and 3 John to an individual).

James

This letter was written by "James, a servant of God and of the Lord Jesus Christ" (Jas. 1:1). Tradition indicates this was James the Just, Jesus' "brother" (Gal. 1:19). The letter is addressed to "the twelve tribes in the Dispersion" (Jas. 1:1), indicating a wide audience of Jewish Christians in the nations where they were scattered (see Acts 26:7).

The letter focuses on ethical teaching, echoing many points in the Gospels, particularly Matthew's Sermon on the Mount (Matt. 5–7).

James the Just was martyred in A.D. 62,[41] indicating that the letter was written before then. Its content suggests it was written quite early, though likely after early reports of Paul's First Missionary Journey to the Gentiles had begun to be received at Jerusalem (ca. A.D. 48). This is suggested by its discussion of justification by faith in relationship to works (Jas. 2:14–26), and it points to a composition around A.D. 48, though a later date is not impossible.

If the early date is accurate, the letter of James could be the first book of the New Testament that was written.

1–2 Peter

St. Peter's first letter is addressed to "the exiles of the Dispersion in Pontus, Galatia, Cappadocia, Asia, and Bithynia" (1 Pet. 1:1)—all parts of modern Turkey. The reference to "the exiles of the Dispersion" could be taken as a reference to Jewish Christians, but there are indications that Peter has Gentiles in mind (1 Pet. 1:18; 2:10; 3:6; 4:3–4). It was likely written not long before 2 Peter, perhaps around A.D. 62–63. The letter was written from Rome, which Peter refers to with the codename "Babylon" (1 Pet. 5:13). Its purpose was to exhort Christians to live lives of faith and obedience.

Second Peter doesn't identify where its audience lived, but it refers to itself as "the second letter I have written you," indicating the same audience as 1 Peter. It is, therefore, also later, and since Peter says he knows his death will be soon

(2 Pet. 1:12–15), it was likely written around A.D. 64–65, shortly before his martyrdom in 65 or 66.

The purpose of the letter was to exhort Christians to remain faithful, to lead moral lives, to await the coming of the Lord, and to avoid false teachers, including those who were perverting the writings of St. Paul (2 Pet. 3:15–17).

Some in the early Church had doubts about whether 2 Peter was authentic, but under the guidance of the Holy Spirit, the Catholic Church ultimately included it in the canon of Scripture.

1–3 John

Three of the catholic epistles are attributed to St. John. The first was recognized early on as Scripture, but some had doubts about the second two.

First John is similar to Hebrews in that it lacks standard features of a letter (sender, recipients, greeting), making it read more like a homily. Its purpose is pastoral, and John exhorts his readers to live as Christians should and to avoid certain false teachers who have withdrawn from the community (1 John 2:18–23).

It shows notable similarities to the Gospel of John. Not only is the style similar, it also shares many of the same themes (being born of God, the new commandment of love, light and darkness). The opening of the letter (1 John 1:1–7) is strongly reminiscent of the opening of the Gospel (John 1:1–9). External tradition consequently attributes it to the same author as the Gospel.

Second John is only a single chapter long. It is written by "the elder," whom external tradition identifies as John, though there is a question of whether it is John, son of Zebedee, or John the Elder, an eyewitness of Jesus' ministry mentioned by several early Church Fathers.

The letter is addressed to "the elect lady and her children." In keeping with the early practice of personifying churches as women (see 1 Pet. 5:13), scholars have understood this as a reference to a local church and its members. The elder encourages the readers to love one another and guard against "men who will not acknowledge the coming of Jesus Christ in the flesh; such a one is the deceiver and the Antichrist" (2 John 1:7).

Third John is the shortest book of the New Testament, being just 218 words in Greek. It is from the elder to a man named Gaius. The elder commends him for serving fellow Christians, including traveling missionaries (vv. 5–8). He also warns against a man named Diotrephes, who was critical of the elder and refused to welcome others from the elder's circle (vv. 9–10).

This letter may be a companion to 2 John since the elder says he has "written something to the church" (v. 9). Gaius may have been a leader in the church to which 2 John was written.

None of the three letters contains concrete indications of when they were written, so scholars have generally placed them in the same period as the other books attributed to John. Most commonly, they are placed in the A.D. 90s, but on our estimation it should be the 60s.

Jude

Jude is a single chapter long. Its sender is "Jude, a servant of Jesus Christ and brother of James." The use of the name James without qualification points to the most famous James of the time—that is, James the Just. This makes the author one of the "brethren" of the Lord (see Mark 6:3). The letter was written for a very specific purpose: to warn against false teachers and their immoral lifestyle.

Jude's letter likely was written after James's death in A.D. 62 when Jude would have assumed a more prominent role and been more likely to write a letter with as broad an audience as this one: "those who are called, beloved in God the Father and kept for Jesus Christ" (v. 1). It also was written when those who heard the apostles were still alive (v. 17).

Jude and 2 Peter have a great deal of overlap (cf. Jude 6–13 and 2 Peter 2:4–17). The parallels are so close that either one must be borrowing from the other, or there must be a common source behind the two. Without a way of resolving this matter, we date Jude to approximately the same time as 2 Peter—that is, around A.D. 64–65, though it could have been earlier or later.

THE BOOK OF REVELATION

The final book in a modern Bible is Revelation. Its purpose is "to show to [Christ's] servants what must soon take place; and he made it known by sending his angel to his servant John" (Rev. 1:1). Revelation encourages Christians to hold fast to their faith in the face of persecution and the traumatic events that were soon to come.

Most have understood the author to be John, son of Zebedee, though some, both in the early Church and today, understood it to be John the Elder.[42] Some in the early Church also questioned whether it should be counted as Scripture, but the Holy Spirit led the Catholic Church to conclude that it is.

Revelation is addressed to "the seven churches that are in Asia" (Rev. 1:4)—that is, Ephesus, Smyrna, Pergamum, Thyatira, Sardis, Philadelphia, and Laodicea (Rev. 1:11). There were actually more churches in the province of Asia Minor at the time (e.g., Colossae), but these seven are likely selected both because John was personally familiar with them and because seven is a biblical symbol for completeness.

The book was written while John was in exile on the island of Patmos (Rev. 1:9). This doesn't mean Patmos was a penal colony (it wasn't), but it was common to exile troublesome people to islands to keep them out of important cities.

Many have dated the book to the 90s, but there is evidence it was written earlier. It speaks of the Jerusalem temple as still operating (Rev. 11:1–2). The most precise clue to its dating may the interpretation it gives of the seven heads of the beast that John sees: "The seven heads are seven mountains on which the woman is seated; they are also seven kings, five of whom have fallen, one is, the other has not yet come, and when he comes he must remain only a little while" (Rev. 17:9–10).

The seven mountains have been identified since ancient times as the seven hills of Rome, and so the seven kings involve a reference to Roman emperors. Note that—like the Roman emperors—the beast blasphemes God, persecutes the saints, rules the world, and receives worship from all but Christians (Rev. 13:6–8). It also has the number 666 (Rev. 13:18), which is what "Nero Caesar" (NRWN QSR) adds up to in Hebrew and Aramaic (N+R+W+N+Q+S+R = 50+200+6+50+100+60+200 = 666).

If the seven heads are the line of first-century emperors, the five who "have fallen" would be Augustus, Tiberius, Caligula, Claudius, and Nero. The one who "is" would be Nero's successor, Galba, and the other who "has not yet come" would be Otho, who did indeed reign "only a little while" (three months). This would place the composition of Revelation during the reign of Galba (June 9, 68–January 15, 69).

OTHER FIRST-CENTURY WORKS

The New Testament books weren't the only Christian books written in the Apostolic Age. Many have not survived, but some have. These include:

- *The Didache*: A church manual giving basic instruction on morality, the sacraments, prayer, church officers, and prophecy. It likely appeared in more than one edition, but the earliest was written when there were traveling apostles and prophets because the document includes instructions on how to tell true ones from false ones.

- *The Ascension of Isaiah*: A work set in the time of Isaiah. It describes his martyrdom and contains a vision in which he ascends through the seven heavens as well as prophecies about Jesus and the early Church. Internal clues suggest it was written after Peter's martyrdom but before Nero's suicide, suggesting a date around A.D. 67.

- *1 Clement*: A letter by Pope St. Clement I. It helped settle a conflict at Corinth. Although often dated to the A.D. 90s, the evidence suggests an earlier date. It was written just after the city of Rome had experienced a series of "sudden and successive calamitous events" (chap. 1), after Peter and Paul's martyrdoms (chap. 5), but before the destruction of the Jerusalem temple (chap. 41). That likely places it in the first half of A.D. 70 after the disastrous "year of four emperors" that took place in 69 but before the destruction of the temple in August of 70.

- *The Letter of Barnabas*: An early document offering a spiritual interpretation of Jewish law and customs and how they are fulfilled in Christ and the Church. Scholars generally don't think it was by the biblical Barnabas. It was written shortly after the destruction of the Jerusalem temple (chap. 16), perhaps around A.D. 75.

- *The Shepherd of Hermas*: A collection of visions by a former slave named Hermas who lived in the city of Rome during the time of Pope St. Clement I. The visions deal with virtue, forgiveness, and the need to repent. He began receiving them perhaps around A.D. 80.

- *The Odes of Solomon*: A collection of forty-two hymns used in the early Church. They were probably composed around the year 100.

THE FIRST COLLECTIONS OF NEW TESTAMENT BOOKS

How did the New Testament begin to come together? The first stage probably involved an early collection of letters.

Books like the Gospels, Acts, and Revelation were long enough that they could comfortably fit in separate scrolls or codices, but this wasn't the case with the letters. They were too short, so it was natural for Christians to begin to publish them in collected editions.

The first such collection would have involved letters by St. Paul.[43] Until recently, many scholars supposed the process by which his letters were collected was a slow one. It was assumed that the only copy in existence of each Pauline letter was held by the church that received it. Over a long period, some of these churches began making copies and circulating them to other churches. This led to the collection we have in the New Testament by an organic process nobody supervised.

But this is not how ancient letter collections normally came about. If an author viewed his letters as having literary merit, he retained copies of the ones he sent for his own archives, and it was from these that letter collections were made.

The first collection was done at the author's initiative. He would go through his archives and select the letters he wanted to publish. Then he would edit them and arrange them for publication according to some plan (e.g., when they were written, to whom they were written, how long they were, what they were about). If the collection proved popular, later editors—often after the original author's death—would produce expanded editions in which they took more letters from the author's archives and added them to the end of the original edition following whatever plan of organization the author had established.

St. Paul definitely considered his letters to be literary works as illustrated by their enormous length, the careful structure and reasoning he put into them, and the costs he paid to have them made. As major literary productions, Paul would have saved copies in his personal archives. He even appears to ask Timothy to bring him those archives toward the end of his life (2 Tim. 4:13).

It's thus likely that the first collected edition of Paul's letters was issued by the apostle himself. Not only was this the standard practice in the ancient world, but we also have external evidence supporting it. When writing to the Corinthians, Clement I refers to 1 Corinthians as what Paul "first" wrote to the church.[44] But we know Paul had written them a previous letter (1 Cor. 5:9). This indicates Clement had encountered 1 Corinthians as the "first" letter to that church in a collection. But Clement is writing in the first half of A.D. 70 just three years after Paul's martyrdom in mid-67. That strongly suggests that the first collection of Paul's letters was produced in the apostle's lifetime.

Similarly, Peter expects his audience to be familiar with multiple Pauline letters (2 Pet. 3:15–16). But they wouldn't be if scattered churches here and there only had a single letter or two and there was no collection in circulation.

We can even tell what the first collection included. This is because of the way Paul's letters are organized. They are in two groups: those written to churches and those written to individuals. Each collection is organized in descending order of length. Romans is the longest letter written to a church, so it comes first, while the letters to the Thessalonians are shortest, and they are last. First Timothy is the longest letter to an individual, while Philemon is the shortest, so they are respectively first and last.

But there is an exception to this pattern. The letter to the Ephesians is longer than Galatians which precedes it. This suggests that the first collection included Romans, 1–2 Corinthians, and Galatians. Later, an expanded collection including Ephesians, Philippians, Colossians, and 1–2 Thessalonians was produced. After his death, one of his companions likely went through the archives and added more letters in descending order of size.

Also, likely at the same time, another collection of his letters to individuals (1–2 Timothy, Titus, and Philemon) was produced and also arranged by size. This third collection takes us up to Paul's death (2 Tim. 4:6–8), so it was probably released after his death, perhaps by Luke or Timothy (2 Tim. 4:11, 21).

What about the catholic epistles? Although written in the Apostolic Age, they were likely collected later. This is shown by the fact they were from different authors who didn't all die at the same time, and by the fact the collection seems to be modeled on other things in the New Testament.

These also are in descending order of size, and early on it was noticed that Paul had written to seven churches or

THE WRITING OF THE NEW TESTAMENT

groups of churches (i.e., those in Rome, Corinth, Galatia, Ephesus, Philippi, Colossae, and Thessalonica). It also was noted that—if you count Hebrews as Pauline—this makes fourteen total letters (two times seven). And it was noted that the book of Revelation is addressed to seven churches (Rev. 1:4, 11).

Seven was considered a holy number, and it is no accident that there are seven catholic epistles, based on the precedent of Paul and Revelation. In fact, this may be why—on the human level—letters as seemingly insignificant as 2 and 3 John were included, though ultimately all of this took place under the guidance of the Holy Spirit.

THE CATHOLIC CHURCH GETS ITS NAME

Around the end of the Apostolic Age, the Catholic Church received the name that it is known by today.

Originally, Christianity was simply called "the Way" (Acts 9:2; 19:23; 22:4; 24:14, 22), a phrase that is short for "the way of salvation" (Acts 16:17), "the way of the Lord" (Acts 18:25), and "the way of God" (Acts 18:26). However, with time followers of Jesus came to be known as "Christians"— a name they were given in the city of Antioch (Acts 11:26).

As long as Christians remained united, they didn't need more specific designations. But as schisms and heresies appeared, faithful Christians needed a way to refer to these groups.

One such group was called the Nicolaitans (Rev. 2:6, 15). They appear to have made compromises with pagan idolatry and sexual immorality. According to second- and third-century sources, they were named after a man named Nicolaus,[45] who may have been one of "the Seven" appointed by the apostles in Acts 6. Some sources say Nicolaus fell into error,[46] though others say people misunderstood and misapplied his teaching.[47]

Other sects also arose. These might be named after their founder (the Marcionites were founded by Marcion of Sinope), after their distinctive doctrine (the Gnostics claimed to have special *gnosis*, "knowledge"), after a distinctive practice (the Encratites practiced excessive *enkrateia* or "self-control" by refusing marriage and meat eating), or after their place of origin (the Phrygian heresy of Montanus arose in Phrygia).

This is similar to how recent groups are named after their founders (Lutheranism was founded by Martin Luther), doctrines (Presbyterians holds that churches should be governed by presbyters), practices (Seventh-day Adventists worship on Saturday, the seventh day), or locations (Anglicanism began in England).

As sects emerged in the early Church, not only did they need names, but the original Church from which they sprang also did. Since this Church was spread over the whole world, it was a universal Church, and so it came to be called *katholikos*, the Greek term for "general" or "universal."

The first surviving reference to the Church using this term is in the letters of St. Ignatius of Antioch. Around A.D. 108, he wrote:

> Let that be considered a valid Eucharist which is celebrated by the bishop, or by one whom he appoints. Wherever the bishop appears let the congregation be present; just as wherever Jesus Christ is, there is the Catholic Church.[48]

The fact that Ignatius uses this term without stopping to explain it could indicate it was already in use, which would place its origin in the late first century.

THE CLOSE OF THE APOSTOLIC AGE

The first apostle to die was St. James, son of Zebedee, who was put to death by King Herod Agrippa I around A.D. 43 (Acts 12:1). Then James the Just was martyred in 62, Peter around 65 or 66, and Paul around 67.

We don't know whom the last apostle to die was, though it's often assumed to be John, son of Zebedee. It is certain that the last apostle died either in the late first or early second century. With this transition, several changes occurred.

First, the era of public revelation ended. From this point forward, there would be no new revelation binding for all Christians. The *Catechism of the Catholic Church* explains:

> The Christian economy, therefore, since it is the new and definitive covenant, will never pass away; and no new public revelation is to be expected before the glorious manifestation of our Lord Jesus Christ (66).

This doesn't mean God no longer gives revelation of any sort:

> Throughout the ages, there have been so-called "private" revelations, some of which have been recognized by the authority of the Church. They do not belong, however, to the deposit of faith. It is not their role to improve or complete Christ's definitive revelation, but to help live more fully by it in a certain period of history. Guided by the Magisterium of the Church, the *sensus fidelium* (Latin, "the sense of the faithful") knows how to discern and welcome in these revelations whatever constitutes an authentic call of Christ or his saints to the Church.

Christian faith cannot accept "revelations" that claim to surpass or correct the revelation of which Christ is the fulfillment, as is the case in certain non-Christian religions and also in certain recent sects which base themselves on such "revelations" (CCC 67).

Second, because the apostles were no longer alive, the leadership of the Catholic Church passed to the next-highest-ranking leaders, the bishops, who succeeded the apostles in governing the Christian community.

In order that the full and living Gospel might always be preserved in the Church the apostles left bishops as their successors. They gave them their own position of teaching authority. Indeed, the apostolic preaching, which is expressed in a special way in the inspired books, was to be preserved in a continuous line of succession until the end of time (CCC 77).

DOCTRINE IN THE APOSTOLIC AGE

Before discussing later periods, we should consider how Christians in the Apostolic Age formed their beliefs. Like us, they couldn't simply make things up. They were bound to heed the revelation that God provided. That revelation was found both in the books of Scripture and in the Sacred Tradition handed down by Jesus and the apostles.

Christians in this period thus used a Scripture-plus-Tradition model. Also, to make sure they understood the contents of Scripture and Tradition correctly, they relied on the Church's divinely guided and authoritative teachers—the group we now refer to as the Magisterium (Latin, *magister*, "teacher"). This group originally consisted of the apostles, but when they passed from the scene, it was inherited by their successors, the bishops.

According to the Catholic Church, we should use the same model the first Christians did: we need to rely on Scripture and Tradition as the sources of publicly binding revelation, and we need to rely on the Magisterium—the bishops teaching in union with the pope—to ensure we have understood them correctly.

However, in recent centuries, members of the Protestant community have proposed a different model. They say we should obtain doctrine *sola scriptura* (Latin, "by Scripture alone") and refuse to give Tradition and the Magisterium an authoritative role.

If this idea were true, if we had to prove every doctrine by Scripture alone, then we would have to prove the doctrine of *sola scriptura* this way. In other words, *sola scriptura* would need to meet its own test. We would need to prove—by appealing *only* to Scripture—that we are to exclude Tradition and the Magisterium from having authoritative roles.

What kind of Bible verses would be able to prove that? Not just any verse will do. Since we know the apostles expected Christians to regard Scripture, Tradition, and their own teaching (acts of the Magisterium) as authoritative during the Apostolic Age, we'd need verses that speak of a time *after* the Apostolic Age. We would need verses that say things like, "We apostles have agreed to ensure that everything authoritative gets written down in Scripture, so once we are gone, don't treat anything else as authoritative" or "Even though something we've taught *you* is authoritative, it will cease to be authoritative once we pass from the scene."

Needless to say, there are no such verses. It was a common view in the first century that Jesus would return during the lives of the apostles (see John 21:21–23; Acts 1:6; 1 Thess.

4:17). Only a few passages in the New Testament show any awareness that the Apostolic Age may be passing (2 Tim. 4:6; 2 Pet. 1:14) or that there will be a further age before the end (Rev. 20:1–5). None of these passages indicate there is to be a shift in how Christians obtain doctrine or that Tradition and the Magisterium will suddenly lose their authority. The logical conclusion, as the Catholic Church maintains, is that they are still authoritative.

4

After the New Testament

THE WORD OF GOD IN THE EARLY CHURCH

Christians continued writing after the age of the apostles, and as the number of Christians grew, so did the number of Christian books.

Many of the writings produced in this period were by a group of individuals known as the Church Fathers. To qualify as a Father, an individual needs to have four characteristics: antiquity, orthodoxy, holiness, and approval by the Church:

- *Antiquity* refers to the age in which he lived. The age of the Fathers covers the period from the first century through to the time of St. Isidore of Seville in the-West (died 636) and St. John of Damascus in the East (died ca. 749).

- *Orthodoxy* means he had to teach the Christian faith correctly as it was expressed in his day. This doesn't mean that he had to use language or concepts formulated in later ages. But it does mean he had to teach the fundamentals of the Faith accurately, given the level of doctrinal development that had occurred by his day.

- *Holiness* is indicated if the person is recognized as a saint. The Latin term for *saint*—*sanctus*—means "holy."
- *Approval by the Church* is somewhat tricky because there is no formal list of writers who have been approved as Fathers. However, if an individual is a saint, this indicates fundamental Church approval.

Authors who lack one or more of these qualities aren't referred to as Fathers but as "ecclesiastical" (Church) writers. For example, one important early Christian author was Tertullian of Carthage (ca. 157–ca. 245). He lived in the right period to be a Father, but he never became a saint because of his support for a sect known as the Montanists. Therefore, he is only an ecclesiastical writer.

SECOND-CENTURY BOOKS

Writers after the Apostolic Age used many types of documents to communicate the Faith: letters, homilies, commentaries on biblical books, and theological treatises.

A form that became especially important in the second century was the apology (Greek, *apologia*)—a defense of the Christian faith offered to non-Christians, either pagans or Jews. For example, St. Justin Martyr wrote a famous defense of the Christian Faith for the Roman emperor Antonius Pius in the A.D. 150s.

Christians wrote books in second century that are similar to the books of the New Testament. Some took the form of historical narratives similar to the four Gospels and Acts, letters like those of the apostles, and books of prophecy like Revelation.

The works similar to the Gospels focused on Jesus and sought to fill in pieces of his life that Christians were naturally curious about. One such work is known as the *Protoevangelium of James*. *Protoevangelium* means "first gospel," and this work is also known as the *Infancy Gospel of James*. It describes the events leading up to the birth of Christ focusing on the life of the Virgin Mary. This work shouldn't be considered historically reliable, but it's very early and may contain some authentic memories of Jesus' family. For example, it offers the earliest explanation of who the "brothers" of Jesus were, indicating Joseph was an elderly widower who already had a family. This is why he was willing to become the guardian of a consecrated virgin like Mary. She thus remained a virgin her entire life, and the "brothers" of Jesus were said to be step-brothers through Joseph.

Other narratives followed the model of Acts. Around A.D. 160, a priest from the province of Asia was a great admirer of St. Paul and wrote a book known as the *Acts of Paul*. It is a kind of sequel to Acts. Again, it isn't historically reliable, but it may contain some authentic traditions about the apostle. For example, it contains a famous description of Paul as "a man small in size, baldheaded, bandy-legged, well-built, with eyebrows meeting, rather long-nosed, full of grace." Since this description isn't particularly flattering, it wasn't made up to glorify Paul and may be an accurate memory of what he looked like.

Some writers composed letters modeled after those of Paul. The *Acts of Paul* contains a "third" letter to the Corinthians. The early centuries also saw the publication of a supposed letter to the Laodiceans (to supply the lost one referred to in Col. 4:16) as well as a collection of letters supposedly exchanged by Paul and the famous Roman philosopher Seneca.

Finally, some early Christian books were similar to Revelation. In the A.D. 130s, a work known as the *Revelation of Peter* (also called the *Apocalypse of Peter*) was penned. It contained prophecies about Israel as well as descriptions of hell and heaven.

While not authentic or historically accurate, books like these were in circulation among orthodox Christians. They were certainly popular, or there wouldn't have been enough copies for them to survive (though we have only portions of the *Acts of Paul*).

It's hard to know what people thought about them. Some may have been seen as simply exercises in Christian imagination—much like authors today write historical novels to help people imagine what it was like in Bible times. But in some cases, at least a few people took them to be Scripture. Thus, some in the early Church looked on the *Revelation of Peter* as a work of Scripture to be read alongside the Revelation of John.

Unfortunately, some works of this period were penned by heretics. Around A.D. 140, a man named Marcion came to Rome and claimed that the God of Judaism isn't the same God that Christians worship. He thus rejected the Old Testament and produced a mutilated edition of the New Testament that cut out parts he viewed as too Jewish. Marcion's New Testament included an edited version of the Gospel of Luke and a pared-down collection of ten of Paul's letters.

A group known as the Gnostics wrote many false scriptures. There were various kinds of Gnostics, but they all claimed to have special revealed knowledge (Greek, *gnôsis*). Their views varied, but they generally claimed that the true, ultimate God was unknowable, that the material world was evil, and that it was created by an inferior being known as the Demiurge (Greek, *demiurgos*, "craftsman"). In the second and third centuries, many gnostic scriptures were written, including the *Gospel of Thomas,* the *Apocryphon of John*, and the *Apocryphon of James*.

The production of these false scriptures contributed to the formation of the biblical canon.

THE BIBLE BEGINS TO COME TOGETHER

As the number of Christian books grew, so did the need for the Catholic Church to discern which were truly authoritative, which were merely helpful, and which were positively harmful. This resulted in a process that gradually clarified which books did and didn't count as Scripture.

The guiding principle for Christians was Jesus Christ himself, so the question became which books he would consider authoritative. Since he presented his ministry as the fulfillment of Old Testament prophecy, this meant the Old Testament was Scripture. Like most Jews, Jesus recognized a range of works beyond the Pentateuch as Scripture, but we have no record of him providing a list of them.

Christians, therefore, turned to Jesus' appointed teachers—the apostles—for guidance. In their own writings, the apostles overwhelmingly used the Greek Septuagint translation of the Old Testament, so Christians naturally adopted the Septuagint. The apostles hadn't warned Christians away from any of the Septuagint's books, so the Christian community used the entire Septuagint tradition, which at this time had blurred boundaries.

Jesus made the apostles authoritative teachers in their own right, so their writings could also be recognized as Scripture, as could the writings of men the apostles trusted, allowing Peter's companion Mark and Paul's companion Luke to write Gospels. But there were limits to who could author Scripture, and this gift ceased with the close of the Apostolic Age. No new Scripture was written after this time.

All this gave the Catholic Church general principles for identifying which books could be Scripture, but it didn't settle the question regarding which particular books belonged in the Bible.

So how did the Holy Spirit guide the Church into recognizing the canonicity of particular books?

THE ROLE OF TRADITION

The answer involved Tradition. When the New Testament authors originally gave their books to the Church, it was with the understanding that they were authoritative for the Faith. The evangelists, St. Paul, and the others didn't view themselves as simply making suggestions or proposing ideas. They saw themselves as passing on authoritative teachings of the Christian faith to their congregations.

A key way this happened was through the liturgy. Since most people were illiterate and could not afford their own copies of the scriptures, they depended on hearing them read in church. In the A.D. 150s, Justin Martyr describes a typical Christian liturgy and notes it involved reading "the memoirs of the apostles or the writings of the prophets," after which the congregation would be instructed to apply these to their lives:

> On the day which is called Sunday we have a common assembly of all who live in the cities or in the outlying districts, and the memoirs of the apostles or the writings of the prophets are read, as long as there is time. Then, when the reader has finished, the president of the assembly verbally admonishes and invites all to imitate such examples of virtue. Then we all stand up together and offer up our prayers, and, as we said before, after

we finish our prayers, bread and wine and water are presented. He who presides likewise offers up prayers and thanksgivings, to the best of his ability, and the people express their approval by saying "Amen." The eucharistic elements are distributed and consumed by those present, and to those who are absent they are sent through the deacons.[49]

The congregations received the books handed down from the apostles on the understanding that they are authoritative. They knew and trusted the New Testament authors. Indeed, they had entrusted their eternal souls to their teachings. Consequently, they accepted the New Testament books in faith and handed them on in the churches as authoritative.

A tradition was stablished that these books were the genuine article. In the case of many, the tradition spread so quickly and strongly that there was never any doubt among Christians about their status. Thus, people never doubted the inclusion of books like Matthew or Romans in the canon.

But in the case of some books, particularly some of the shorter ones and ones written later, the tradition concerning them didn't have a chance to fully mature by the end of the Apostolic Age. Consequently, in later years there was a division of opinion about Hebrews, James, 2 Peter, 2 and 3 John, Jude, and Revelation. These are occasionally referred to as the *antilegomena* because they were sometimes disputed or "spoken against" (Greek, *anti-*, "against" + *legô,* "speak").

On the other hand, certain books were written early enough and were connected closely enough with the apostles that some thought them Scripture even though they weren't ultimately included in the New Testament.

Some considered the *Letter of Barnabas* canonical. Since Clement of Rome was an associate of the apostles, some considered *1 Clement* canonical. And others regarded the work of first-century prophetic book *The Shepherd of Hermas* to be Scripture. Each of these figures was identified as an apostle (see Acts 14:14) or the associate of an apostle (see Rom. 16:14; Phil. 4:3).

When it came to the books clearly written after the Apostolic Age, Tradition played the reverse role: rather than providing an argument to include them, it was an argument to exclude them. When a new book appeared, the questions would be asked, "If this book is apostolic, why is there no tradition concerning it? Where are the churches that can vouch for its being authentic and that have been reading it in their liturgies all this time?" The absence of such a tradition concerning books like the *Protoevangelium of James* and the *Acts of Paul* is one reason they were not included in the New Testament.

Tradition played another role in excluding books. Many of the books written in the second and subsequent centuries were heretical and contradicted the teachings handed down from Christ and the apostles. Such books *could not* be from the apostles or their approved associates. The fact that works like the *Apocryphon of John* and the *Apocryphon of James* taught gnostic heresies that contradicted the apostolic Tradition, together with the fact there was no tradition of their being read in the Church's liturgy, is why they were immediately recognized as fakes.

Thus, Tradition was the crucial factor in discerning whether a book belonged in Scripture: the tradition that a book was authentic and authoritative was reason to include it, and it was to be excluded if there was the absence of such a tradition or if it positively contradicted apostolic Tradition.

STAGES IN THE PROCESS

As the Holy Spirit guided the Catholic Church, the boundaries of the canon became firmer. Still, this process took time. Early in the 300s, Bishop Eusebius of Caesarea wrote his famous *Church History* in which he described the state of views in his own day.[50] He divided the books into several categories:

Accepted books:

- The Gospels of Matthew, Mark, Luke, and John
- Acts
- The letters of Paul
- 1 John
- 1 Peter

Disputed books:

- Letter to the Hebrews
- James
- 2 Peter
- 2–3 John
- Jude
- Revelation of John (listed by some as accepted, by others as rejected)
- *Shepherd of Hermas* (also listed by some as accepted, by others as rejected)
- *Gospel of the Hebrews*

Rejected books:

- *Revelation of Peter*
- *Letter of Barnabas*

- *The Didache*
- *Gospels of Peter, Thomas, and Matthias*
- *Acts of Paul, Andrew, and John*

By the late 300s, the situation had become even clearer. In 382, Pope Damasus I held a council at Rome that discussed the biblical canon. It stated:

> Now indeed we must treat of the divine scriptures, what the universal Catholic Church accepts and what she must avoid.
>
> At the beginning, the order of the Old Testament. Genesis, one book; Exodus, one book; Leviticus, one book; Numbers, one book; Deuteronomy, one book; Joshua, one book; Judges, one book; Ruth, one book; Kings, four books [i.e., two books of Samuel, two books of Kings]; Chronicles, two books; 150 Psalms, one book; three books of Solomon; Proverbs, one book; Ecclesiastes, one book; Song of Songs, one book; likewise, Wisdom, one book; Ecclesiasticus [i.e., Sirach], one book.
>
> Likewise, the order of the prophets. Isaiah, one book; Jeremiah, one book, along with the *Qinoth*, that is, his Lamentations; Ezekiel, one book; Daniel, one book; Hosea, one book; Amos, one book; Micah, one book; Joel, one book; Obadiah, one book; Jonah, one book; Nahum, one book; Habakkuk, one book; Zephaniah, one book; Haggai, one book; Zechariah, one book; Malachi, one book.
>
> Likewise, the order of the histories. Job, one book; Tobit, one book; Ezra, two books [i.e., Ezra and Nehemiah]; Esther, one book; Judith, one book; of the Maccabees, two books.
>
> Likewise, the order of the scriptures of the New and eternal Testament, which the holy and Catholic Church

accepts. [Four books] of the Gospels: according to Matthew, one book; according to Mark, one book; according to Luke, one book; according to John, one book.

Fourteen letters of Paul: to the Romans, one [letter]; to the Corinthians, two [letters]; to the Ephesians, one; to the Thessalonians, two; to the Galatians, one; to the Philippians, one; to the Colossians, one; to Timothy, two; to Titus, one; to Philemon, one; to the Hebrews, one.

Likewise, one book of the Apocalypse of John [i.e., Revelation].

And one book of the Acts of the Apostles.

Likewise, seven canonical letters: of the apostle Peter, two letters; of the apostle James, one letter; of the apostle John, one letter; of the other John the Presbyter, two letters; of the apostle Jude the Zealot, one letter.[51]

Except for the fact that it doesn't mention Baruch—which was often treated as part of Jeremiah—this is the same list that would later be infallibly affirmed by the Catholic Church. This list was also affirmed by Pope Innocent I in A.D. 405,[52] and it was endorsed by various local councils, including the Council of Hippo of 393, the Council of Carthage of 397, and the Council of Carthage of 419.[53]

These decrees were not infallible. As a result, one could find individuals who questioned or denied the canonicity of certain books—especially the deuterocanonicals.

JEROME AND THE DEUTEROCANONICALS

One of those individuals was St. Jerome (ca. 347–420). However, his attitude is ambiguous and may have changed over time. While learning to translate Hebrew, Jerome was in contact with non-Christian Jews who were the intellectual descendants of Pharisees and, therefore, rejected the deuterocanonicals.

Under this influence, he questioned their canonicity. This is indicated in his prologues to the Vulgate, where he says certain books are non-canonical (e.g., he says this of Wisdom, Sirach, Judith, and Tobit in the prologue to Kings). In other cases, he says a book is not read among Hebrew-speaking Jews but doesn't clearly state his own view (e.g., he says this of Baruch in the prologue to Jeremiah).

Nevertheless, Jerome shows deference to the judgment of the Church. In the prologue to Judith, he tells his patrons that "because this book is found by the Nicene Council [of A.D. 325] to have been counted among the number of the sacred scriptures, I have acquiesced to your request (or should I say demand!)" to translate it. This is interesting because we have only partial records of First Nicaea, and we don't otherwise know what this ecumenical council said concerning the canon.

Jerome's deference to the Church is also illustrated by his defense of the deuterocanonical portions of Daniel. He wrote: "What sin have I committed in following the judgment of the churches?"[54] In the same place, he stated that what he said concerning Daniel in his prologues was what non-Christian Jews said but that it was not his own view. This may indicate that Jerome changed his mind or that his reporting of Jewish views doesn't indicate his own opinion.

Jerome's deference to the Church is correct. The guidance of the Holy Spirit is given to the Church as a whole. No one Father, however prominent, can settle the canon of Scripture, and on this subject Jerome was in the minority.

Despite his ambiguous attitude toward the deuterocanonicals, Jerome did perform an extremely valuable service for the Church.

THE VULGATE

The New Testament was written in Greek, which was the main international language. It was even widely spoken in Rome, where Latin was the native tongue. With time, Latin became more prominent in parts of the empire, and there was a need to translate the Bible into it.

This was done in an informal way, producing what is known as the *Old Latin Version*—a collection of translations of varying quality. Consequently, in 383, Pope Damasus I commissioned Jerome to revise the existing translations and improve them.

In principio creavit Deus cælum et terram. Terra autem erat inanis et vacua, et tenebræ erant super faciem abyssi: et spiritus Dei ferebatur super

First lines of Genesis in Latin

The task took Jerome twenty years, and the result was a much better Latin version that came to be known as the Vulgate because it was in common use (Latin, *vulgata*, "common"). Its influence has been enormous. Protestant biblical scholar Bruce Metzger writes:

Whether one considers the Vulgate from a purely secular point of view, with its pervasive influence on the development of Latin into Romance languages, or whether one has in view only the specifically religious influence, the extent of its penetration into all areas of Western culture is almost beyond calculation. The theology and the devotional language typical of the Roman Catholic Church were either created or transmitted by the Vulgate. Both Protestants and Roman Catholics are heirs of terminology that Jerome either coined or baptized with fresh significance—words such as salvation, regeneration, justification, sanctification, propitiation, reconciliation, inspiration, Scripture, sacrament, and many others.[55]

While the Vulgate became the standard translation of the Bible in the West, the Septuagint Old Testament and the Greek New Testament remained the standard versions in the East.

THE MIDDLE AGES—A TIME OF LEARNING

Despite their undeserved reputation as the "dark ages," the Middle Ages were a time of enormous learning and scholarship. Stretching from around A.D. 500 to 1500, the era saw the careers of numerous scholars still famous today, including:

- The Venerable Bede
- St. Anselm of Canterbury
- St. Bernard of Clairvaux
- Peter Lombard
- St. Albert the Great
- St. Bonaventure
- St. Thomas Aquinas
- William of Ockham

Together, they made incalculable contributions to biblical studies, theology, philosophy, and other fields.

This period saw the emergence of the first universities, which were founded in the 1000s to bring together scholars from multiple disciplines. The university system revolutionized the development and distribution of knowledge, and it has played a key role in every subsequent phase of history, with universities appearing in every culture across the globe.

Universities grew out of the cathedral and monastery schools of the Middle Ages, where monks and nuns taught. Clerics, therefore, performed key roles as professors at the new universities. For example, St. Thomas Aquinas taught at both the University of Paris and the University of Naples.

Scholars in this period wrote numerous commentaries on the books of the Bible as well as theologies setting forth its teachings, putting them in systematic order, and exploring their implications. It was a period of vigorous intellectual exchange with universities holding public debates on theological questions of all sorts.

THE BIBLE IN THE MIDDLE AGES

This flowering of Christian intellectual activity centered on the Bible as the revealed word of God. By this point, bookmakers were skilled enough that all its books could be bound in a single volume, but producing Bibles was difficult.

The printing press hadn't yet been invented, so each copy had to be written out by hand. It required *hundreds* of hours to patiently copy the sacred text. Even if a person were able to carefully copy one verse a minute, it would take almost 600 hours of work to write the 35,500 verses in a Catholic Bible.

In reality, it would take far longer, for it was common to prepare illuminated manuscripts. These were a way of honoring God's word by preparing it in an especially beautiful manner. Not only would the text be carefully copied by hand in neat calligraphy, it would be supplemented by decorative designs and hand-painted illustrations. A key stage of illumination was burnishing, in which gold leaf was applied to the illustrations to make them come alive with reflected light.

Preparing an illuminated manuscript was a complex, multistage process that involved multiple people. The physical pages—typically made of parchment from animal skins—were produced. What would appear on the page was planned. The page would be lined with a ruler to maintain an even flow of text. Someone wrote the text in ink using a reed or quill pen. The illustrations were sketched. Gold leaf was applied. The images were painted with additional colors, and ink borders were supplied to complete the illumination. Through this difficult and complex process, scribes produced works of art that glorified God and are still treasured by art historians today.

A page from an illuminated manuscript

Initially, the scribes who performed this labor were monks, and monasteries often had a room known as a *scriptorium* that was designed to allow multiple monks to pursue the craft uninterrupted. The demand for Bibles was so great, however, that eventually laymen who lived near the monasteries and nuns in their monasteries were trained as scribes.

Such Bibles were fantastically expensive. As had always been the case in the days before the printing press, only individuals who were wealthy could afford personal copies. But institutions like churches, monasteries, and convents possessed them, and the scriptures were read aloud to the faithful at Mass.

Given the expense of producing a Bible, it's no surprise that churches took security precautions to keep them safe. They often were chained to prevent people from stealing them, ensuring they would be available to nourish the faith of the entire community.

Ironically, this fact became the basis of a charge among anti-Catholics that in the Middle Ages the Church "chained the Bible"—implying it was chained to *keep* the people from reading it. Actually, the situation was the opposite: it was chained to ensure people *would* have access to the word of God!

CHAPTER AND VERSE

An important development in biblical scholarship was the introduction of chapter divisions. Modern readers are so familiar with chapters and verses that they often don't realize these weren't there from the beginning.

The only biblical book that naturally has chapters is the Psalms because each psalm is a separate hymn. That means that in a modern Bible, Psalms naturally has 150 chapters. However, the other biblical books originally didn't have such divisions.

Over time, they began to be added. Jewish copies of the Old Testament were frequently divided into paragraphs. In both Jewish and Christian circles, the portions used in the liturgy were divided into sections so they could be read aloud to the faithful at the appropriate times in the year.

However, there was no standard, universal way of dividing the text in Bibles. Individuals began to experiment with chapter divisions, and the system that stuck was created by Stephen Langton (ca. 1150–1228), the Catholic archbishop of Canterbury.

The chapter divisions allowed people to more easily cite and look up passages. No longer would commentators have to say things like, "Isaiah speaks of the Suffering Servant toward the end of his book." Now they could say, "Isaiah speaks of the Suffering Servant in chapter 53."

Eventually, verses also would be introduced. The modern system of verses came from the Protestant Frenchman Robert Estienne (1503–1599), when he published an edition containing them in 1551.

THE BIBLE IN THE AGE OF PRINT

The world was forever altered by the labors of Catholic inventor Johannes Gutenberg (ca. 1400–1468). Born in the German city of Mainz, he developed the modern printing press. Previously, woodblock printing was known in Europe, but it was clumsy and each wood block had to be hand-carved.

A goldsmith, Gutenberg was skilled in working metal, and he developed a hand mold that allowed durable, identical copies of individual letters to be cast. These then could be arranged and rearranged as movable type. No longer would you have to carve a wooden block for a page of text. You could simply select the letters you needed from a stock of existing punches, arrange them in a frame, and you had what you needed to print a page of text.

When Gutenberg introduced his version of the printing press around 1439, it introduced a new age in human communications, the greatest innovation since the invention of writing thousands of years earlier!

Etching of Gutenberg's late-15th-century printing press

Given Catholic reverence for the word of God, the first complete book to be published using the printing press was a two-volume edition of Jerome's Latin Vulgate. It appeared around 1454, and today it is known as the Gutenberg Bible. Copies of the Gutenberg Bible are highly valued. Only a few dozen have survived, and institutions pay millions of dollars for the historic work.

Although a copy of the Gutenberg Bible is costly now, the invention of movable type dramatically lowered the price of books. The printing press was a disruptive technology that shook up the economy. Much like many of inventions of the twentieth century, it made it possible to obtain things for only a fraction of the previous cost. It no longer took long periods to laboriously hand-copy a page of text. Now, once type for the page had been set, copies could be made in moments.

This cut the cost of producing books dramatically, as did new, inexpensive paper, which was becoming popular. The printing press was so superior to previous bookmaking methods that demand for books grew explosively, and within a few decades there were hundreds of printing presses in Europe producing millions of volumes.

THE PRINTING PRESS AND THE PROTESTANT REFORMATION

Every disruptive technology has good qualities, which is why people rush to adopt it. But as the twentieth century also showed us, new technologies also have downsides.

As the excitement over the new, inexpensive books grew, an idea began to develop that wouldn't have been thinkable before this point in history.

In Germany, Martin Luther (1483–1546) was having a difficult time with Church teaching, particularly on indulgences. In 1517, he published a document known as the *Ninety-Five Theses*, offering propositions about indulgences for academic debate. Soon his objections to Catholic teaching expanded, and he questioned a wide range of doctrines and practices.

Since the Apostolic Age, Christians had seen God's word as being passed down through Sacred Scripture and Sacred Tradition, with Christ's appointed teachers in the Magisterium as the guardians of its correct interpretation.

Luther was rejecting the Church's teachings, and that led him to reject the authority of the Magisterium. He still might have appealed to *both* Scripture and Tradition, but it was quickly pointed out that he was also in conflict with Tradition, so he rejected its authority as well. That left him with Scripture, and he began to advocate a doctrine known as *sola scriptura*: the claim that doctrines must be established "by Scripture alone."

As Luther's teachings began to spread, so did the idea of *sola scriptura*, and this was made possible by the printing press. No longer did one have to be rich to afford a Bible. They were now within the reach of just the moderately well off (though of course the poor couldn't afford them). Early Protestant leaders were keen to read and interpret the Bible for themselves. It must have been an exciting time for them as they looked forward to formulating ideas without authoritative guidance from Tradition or the Magisterium.

Naturally, they recognized that if *sola scriptura* applied to them, it would have to apply to everyone. In principle, everyone should read the Bible and determine for himself what Christian doctrine should be. In practice, that wouldn't work because many people couldn't afford Bibles despite the drop in cost, and many couldn't read.

The Reformers also created barriers restricting the practice of *sola scriptura*. The way Protestantism spread was by converting local government officials and having them declare the area Protestant. If people wanted to remain in the region, they had to be part of the new state churches and uphold its doctrines, whether they were Lutheran, Calvinist, Anglican, or something else. This effectively barred ordinary people from using *sola scriptura* beyond the limits allowed by their state church, and it thus created new, authoritative magisteria composed of local Protestant leaders.

While the Reformers prohibited *sola scriptura* for others, they still needed it to justify their own break with the Church, so they continued to preach it as if no double standard existed. They thus continued proclaiming that each man should read the Bible for himself and use it alone to determine Christian doctrine.

Notice the implications of this: If every man should read the Bible for himself, then every man must have a Bible. To formulate doctrine by Scripture alone, one must have a copy of the scriptures. This was not practically possible even in the Reformers' day, and it would have been utterly unthinkable in any prior age. It was only the invention of the printing press that allowed the price to come down to the point that people of moderate means could afford them.

It's easy to see why the idea of *sola scriptura* became popular when it did and among the people that it did. The Reformers were at least moderately well off and had new printed Bibles, and now the invention of the printing press had made the idea of everyone having his own Bible at least conceivable.

But for all prior Church history, *sola scriptura* was simply an impossibility. This has doctrinal implications because God doesn't ask the impossible. Since *sola scriptura* had never been possible, it had never been God's plan. If it had been, God would have started the Christian age after the invention of the printing press, just as he began giving the Jewish scriptures only after the invention of writing.

Since he didn't choose to do this, we must conclude the Catholic Church is correct and the way of formulating doctrine that has been used ever since the days of the apostles is correct: we are to listen to God's word as found both in Sacred Scripture and Sacred Tradition under the guidance of his authoritative teachers, the Magisterium.

NEW PROTESTANT TRANSLATIONS

If every man is supposed to determine doctrine by Scripture alone, that would mean he not only needs a personal copy of the Bible, but he needs it in a language he can read. So, the Reformers began producing Bible translations in local, vernacular languages, or what was called the vulgar (common) tongue.

The Reformers perceived that access to Protestant Bible translations—coupled with their preaching and literature— would help them make converts, and they were correct. Start distributing a Bible translation you've made, accompany it with your own preaching and literature, and you'll make converts. That's how Catholic missionaries did it as soon as the Christian faith began to spread. That's how the Protestant Reformers did it. And that's how modern groups like the Jehovah's Witnesses do it.

Naturally, the Catholic Church was leery of the new Protestant translations and didn't want people to read them. In the same way today, both Catholics and Protestants are leery of the Jehovah's Witnesses' *New World Translation*. It deliberately distorts and misrepresents what the biblical languages say in support of their doctrine. In particular, it mistranslates the Greek whenever the New Testament affirms the fact that Jesus is God—a doctrine that the witnesses reject. The *New World Translation* also contains prefaces and footnotes that teach Jehovah's Witness doctrines that conflict with the Christian Faith.

For the same reasons, Catholics were leery of Protestant editions of the Bible, and they had reason to be. In his German Bible, Luther famously added the word *alone* to Romans 3:28 in support of his doctrine of justification by faith alone. Now the verse read:

> For we hold that a man is justified by faith alone, apart from works of law.

This word isn't present in the Greek. Although some prior Catholic translators had included it, in the new context created by the Reformation—where "faith alone" was a Protestant rallying cry—its addition to the text created the impression for the ordinary German reader that the Bible was clearly siding with Protestant doctrine. He had no way of knowing that it wasn't in the Greek and that this was a matter of interpretation rather than what the original language required.

Luther also made other changes in his Bible. He removed the deuterocanonical books from among the Old Testament works and placed them in an appendix, adding a heading stating, "These books are not held equal to the scriptures." He similarly placed four New Testament books whose canonicity he questioned—Hebrews, James, Jude, and Revelation—at the end of the New Testament along with a preface that distanced them from "the true and certain chief books of the New Testament." In fact, he included multiple prefaces advocating his understanding of doctrine.

With the Bible itself being turned into a vehicle for advocating Protestant teaching, it was no surprise Catholics took a dim view of this and similar editions and warned the faithful away from them. One couldn't expect Catholics to approve of such editions any more than one could expect Protestants to approve of a Bible translated and supplied with prefaces and notes specifically designed to attack Protestantism!

NEW CATHOLIC TRANSLATIONS

Unfortunately, later anti-Catholics misrepresented the Church's attitude toward anti-Catholic editions of the Bible as if the Church were hostile to the Bible itself.

Sometimes, the extraordinary claim was made—and even today is still sometimes made—that the Catholic Church "hates" the Bible and did all it could to suppress it by keeping it in Latin and forbidding people to read it in their own languages.

A moment's consideration will reveal the absurdity of the hatred charge. Some have replied that if the Church truly hated the Bible, it would have disposed of it before the Reformation ever happened; a pope or council would have simply ordered churches and monasteries to get rid of the Bibles when they were the only ones that had them.

The reality is that no such order would have been given, and even if it had, it would have been disobeyed. The Bible was considered precious—sacred. That's why monks labored so intensively to create beautiful illuminated manuscripts. It was one of the ways they glorified God, and the idea of destroying all the Bibles would have been sacrilege. Every priest, bishop, and pope preached from the Bible constantly and held it to be the word of God. The idea of the Church trying to destroy the Bible would be absurd. It was so precious that even in an economically undeveloped age, monks literally covered it in gold!

What about the charge of keeping it in Latin? In the West, most Bibles were in Latin, but in the East, they were always available in Greek. Furthermore, Latin was still a *living language*. It was used internationally in Western Europe. The educated class—the only people who could read—could read Latin. It was a normal thing for them. That's *why* the Bible was translated into Latin in the first place. The point was to make it accessible to more people by using a language they knew.

As long as Latin was in ordinary use, there wasn't a large demand for translations in other languages. However, that didn't mean there weren't any. In fact, there were, and a few illustrations will make the point.

It's interesting that whenever a major Bible translation appears, it tends to meet with criticism because people aren't used to it. They've been accustomed to hearing—

and regarding as sacred—what is said in an existing translation, so when a new one appears, it is jarring to their ears. St. Jerome initially balked when Pope Damasus I asked him to begin the Vulgate and for this reason. He knew that people used to hearing the Old Latin Version would resist a new edition.

St. Augustine wrote[56] about an incident in which a congregation in North Africa began chanting in protest about how the name of a plant was translated in the Vulgate. Protestant scholar Bruce Metzger writes:

> When the congregation heard that Jonah took shelter from the sun under some ivy (*hedera*), with one accord they shouted, "Gourd, gourd" (*cucurbita*), until the reader reinstated the old word lest there be a general exodus of the congregation!
>
> For his part, Jerome defended his work with forthright vigor, referring on occasion to his detractors as "two-legged asses" or "yelping dogs"—persons who "think that ignorance is identical with holiness." In the course of time, however, opposition to the revision subsided, and the superior accuracy and scholarship of Jerome's version gave it the victory. It was a clear case of the survival of the fittest.
>
> For nearly a thousand years, the Vulgate was used as the recognized text of Scripture throughout Western Europe. It also became the basis of pre-Reformation vernacular scriptures such as Wycliffe's English translation in the fourteenth century, as well as the first printed Bibles in German (1466), Italian (1471), Catalán (1478), Czech (1488), and French (1530).[57]

Note that these translations were appearing *before* the Reformation began and—with the exception of Wycliffe's—

they were published *with* Church approval. The Church didn't have a problem with the Bible being translated into the vernacular.

Many are under the impression that Luther's Bible was the first in German and the King James Version was the first in English, but neither is true. The Bible had been not only translated into German but *printed* in that language by 1466—barely a decade after the Gutenberg Bible appeared.

Translations into German and the dialects that developed into it had existed for centuries. The German alphabet was invented by a missionary named Ulfilas, "the Moses of the Goths," who died around A.D. 382. Like many missionaries, he created the writing system so he could translate the scriptures into the language of the people he was evangelizing. He then translated the entire Bible except for the books of Kings because he thought they dealt with war too much to be good for the warlike Germans he was bringing to Christ.

As the German language developed, translations continued to be made, and parts of many manuscripts have survived the ages. When it comes to printed Bibles, "besides 202 manuscripts, Walther enumerates between 1466 and 1521 eighteen impressions of complete German Bibles, twenty-two of Psalters, and twelve of other parts. Of the eighteen complete Bibles, fourteen are in High German."[58]

People also had long been producing translations into English and the dialects that developed into it. There had been previous translations into Anglo-Saxon, Old English, and Middle English before the King James. Metzger notes:

> Interlinear translations into Old English begin to appear in the ninth and tenth centuries. Among surviving copies of Anglo-Saxon renderings of the Gospels in various dialects

are the famous Lindisfarne Gospels, a Latin manuscript (now in the British Library) written by Bishop Eadfrith of Lindisfarne toward the end of the seventh century. About the middle of the tenth century, a priest named Aldred wrote between the lines a literal rendering of the Latin in the Northumbrian dialect. A similar gloss is provided in the Rushworth Gospels, a manuscript copied from the Lindisfarne Gospels and now housed in the Bodleian Library, Oxford. The Rushworth glosses are practically transcripts of the Lindisfarne glosses so far as the Gospels of Mark, Luke, and John are concerned, but in Matthew the Rushworth gloss is an independent rendering in the rare Mercian dialect by a priest named Farman.[59]

In fact, the major Catholic edition of the Bible in English *preceded* the King James Version. Due to Protestant persecution in England, a group of Catholic scholars fled to France, where they translated the entire Bible into English. Due to limited funding, they initially were able to publish only the New Testament, which appeared in Rheims in 1582. Once they secured additional funding, the Old Testament was published in Douay in 1609–10. Together, these became known as the *Douay-Rheims Version*, and it became the major English translation for Catholics for several centuries.

When the King James Version appeared in 1611, the same resistance that greeted the Vulgate occurred again. People were used to previous English translations, and they didn't immediately like the King James Version. The translators knew this would happen, so they included a preface—"The Translators to the Reader"—to explain and justify why they were issuing a new translation.

The preface makes for fascinating reading because it is clear the King James translators anticipated a great deal of pushback. They were receiving it even before the work was published. They comment:

> Many men's mouths have been open a good while (and yet are not stopped) with speeches about the translation so long in hand, or rather perusals of translations made before: and ask what may be the reason, what the necessity, of the employment. Hath the Church been deceived, say they, all this while?

Many people felt the existing translations were good and that if a new one was to be made, Catholic scholars were the ones best equipped to produce it. The translators describe their critics as arguing:

> Was their translation good before? Why do they now mend it? Was it not good? Why then was it obtruded to the people? Yea, why did the Catholicks (meaning Popish *Romanists*) always go in jeopardy for refusing to go to hear it? Nay, if it must be translated into *English*, Catholicks are fittest to do it. They have learning, and they know when a thing is well.

The translators also provide an extensive discussion of previous Bible translations, praising Jerome for his Vulgate and saying that by making it "he hath forever bound the Church unto him in a debt of special remembrance and thankfulness."

They note that translating the Bible into the vernacular language was the normal procedure whenever a land was evangelized:

> For the behoof [i.e., benefit] and edifying of the unlearned which hungered and thirsted after righteousness, and had

THE BIBLE IS A CATHOLIC BOOK

souls to be saved as well as they, they [i.e., learned people] provided translations into the vulgar for their countrymen, insomuch that most nations under heaven did shortly after their conversion hear *Christ* speaking unto them in their mother tongue, not by the voice of their minister only, but also by the written word translated.

The King James translators then provide an extensive list of translations made for different peoples, including the Syrians, Egyptians, Indians, Persians, Ethiopians, Armenians, Scythians, Goths, Arabs, Saxons, French, Slavonians, and Dutch. They even mention the recently released Douay-Rheims translation and take a swipe at it for using technical terms, saying, "We have shunned the obscurity of the Papists, in their *Azimes, Tunike, Rational, Holocausts, Praepuce, Pasche*, and a number of such like, whereof their late translation is full."

It's easy to take a swipe at a Bible translation for using unfamiliar words. In fact, the King James is often subject to this criticism. But this illustrates our point: far from "hating" the Bible, the Catholic Church had actually been producing translations into English and other languages for centuries, precisely so that people who didn't speak Latin would have access to them!

THE CANON OF SCRIPTURE

Sola scriptura wasn't Luther's only controversial position on the Bible. Another concerned the books that belong to it.

Among the Catholic teachings Luther objected to was the idea of purgatory. Although this can be supported both from the Old and New Testaments, a particularly clear passage is found in 2 Maccabees where Judah Maccabee and his men discover the bodies of fellow Jewish soldiers who had fallen in battle. They found that each of the fallen was wearing a superstitious amulet and concluded this is why they were allowed to perish. However, because they also died fighting for the Lord, they concluded the sin was not irredeemable.

And they turned to prayer, beseeching that the sin which had been committed might be wholly blotted out. And the noble Judas exhorted the people to keep themselves free from sin, for they had seen with their own eyes what had happened because of the sin of those who had fallen.

He also took up a collection, man by man, to the amount of two thousand drachmas of silver, a' [1] sent it to Jerusalem to provide for a sin offering. In doing this he acted very well and honorably, taking account of the resurrection.

For if he were not expecting that those who had fallen would rise again, it would have been superfluous and foolish to pray for the dead. But if he was looking to the splendid reward that is laid up for those who fall asleep in godliness, it was a holy and pious thought. Therefore, he made atonement for the dead, that they might be delivered from their sin (2 Macc. 12:42–45).

This passage strongly endorses the practice of praying for the dead so they might be freed from the consequences of sin, indicating it's possible for the dead to be purified from such consequences; in other words, there is a purgatory.

Luther didn't like this, and his solution was the same as other instances when a source disagreed with him: he rejected its authority. He thus rejected 2 Maccabees as Scripture.

To justify this, Luther's followers appealed to the fact the European Jews with whom they were familiar also rejected it. These were the intellectual descendants of the Pharisees, and they honored a canon of Scripture that was limited to the protocanonical books of the Old Testament. It was reasoned that since the Old Testament books were given to the Jewish people, they were the ones competent to speak to what works belong to it.

One problem with this argument is that European Jews at the time of the Reformation didn't speak for all Jews. Historically, others had accepted the deuterocanonical books. Also, the canon used by European Jews wasn't closed until centuries after the time of Christ. And it clearly was possible for new books of Scripture to be written after the protocanonicals. Otherwise, the New Testament wouldn't be Scripture (something European Jews did, in fact, claim).

Most fundamentally, the Jews whose views counted for Christians weren't those living in sixteenth-century Europe. They were the apostles, who used and quoted the Septuagint without issuing warnings against any of its books. They even used and alluded to the deuterocanonicals. This was why the Church accepted these books in the first place.

Previously, the Church hadn't needed to infallibly define the issue, for there wasn't a widespread attack on the canonicity of the deuterocanonicals, but Protestantism created new urgency to define the canon. Consequently, when the Council of Trent held its fourth session in 1546, it issued an infallible definition that all the books of the Old and New Testament including the deuterocanonicals were sacred and canonical.[60]

This definition also was needed because Luther didn't just reject the deuterocanonical books. He also questioned four New Testament books—Hebrews, James, Jude, and Revelation—which he held did not support his understanding of the gospel. In fact, he famously referred to James, which was hard to reconcile with his ideas about justification by faith alone, as "an epistle of straw" and said he wished he could consign it to the flames.

Later, Protestants weren't willing to go as far as Luther and question books from the New Testament, but they were willing to reject the deuterocanonicals, which they today refer to as the *Apocrypha*. Like Luther's German Bible, early Protestant translations—including the King James—included these books in an appendix, but later many Protestant publishers began dropping the appendix.

Since Trent included the deuterocanonicals in its infallible definition, later anti-Catholics have accused it of "adding" to the Bible. But Trent didn't add anything. It simply reaffirmed the canon the Church had used for centuries going all the way back to the Council of Rome in 382 and the other councils that swiftly followed it. This canon had been reaffirmed as recently as the Council of Florence in 1442.[61] Trent just infallibly endorsed what had long been taught. If anyone was tampering with the recognized canon of Scripture, it was Reformers who were *subtracting* from it by attempting to decanonize certain books of the traditional canon.

Sometimes, Protestants find it incredible that the Church existed so long without an infallible definition of the canon, but the matter simply wasn't urgent until the Reformation. While an individual here or there might disagree, the vast majority accepted the Church's teaching on the canon, and there was no crisis.

But from the Protestant point of view, there is an urgent need to know the precise boundaries of the canon. This need is generated by *sola scriptura*, for if you are to develop doctrine from Scripture alone, it's an urgent priority to know what is and isn't Scripture. If you include even one book in the Bible that *isn't* Scripture, you're feeding false data into your doctrine, and if you omit even one book that *is* Scripture, you're depriving your doctrine of data it's supposed to have.

But if the individual is supposed to rely on the Holy Spirit to guide the Church's Magisterium in the correct interpretation of Scripture and Tradition, there is no intrinsic necessity for every believer to know the precise boundaries of the canon. That's something the Magisterium could always infallibly determine if necessary, and at Trent, it did.

This means a Catholic today can have certainty about the canon, but how is a Protestant—who needs such certainty more than Catholics do—supposed to obtain it? This is a serious problem.

HOW DO WE KNOW WHICH BOOKS ARE SCRIPTURE?

The table of contents in a Bible is not divinely inspired. The authors of the New Testament didn't write a list of the scriptures and hand it down to us. If they had, it would *be* a biblical book, and there never would have been questions about the canon.

So how—on the principle of *sola scriptura*—could a Protestant determine what belongs in the Bible?

Some Protestants argue that the books of the Bible are "self-attesting" as Scripture, but what does this mean? The individual books of the Bible don't say things like, "I am a book of Scripture" or "I am divinely inspired." Even if they did, that wouldn't prove it, for many false scriptures *do* say things of that sort.

Others have supposed that although the books of the Bible don't all claim they are Scripture, they exhibit qualities such as being emotionally inspiring reading that attest to their being Scripture. But what a person finds emotionally inspiring is subjective and varies not only from person to person but even for the same person from time to time. Many find reading the Bible difficult, especially when they first encounter it and aren't used to the biblical authors' styles. Also, they may find other nonbiblical books much more subjectively moving.

It is not possible to name a set of objective literary qualities that show a work is divinely inspired. It also isn't possible to show that the books of the Bible—and these alone—display such qualities. As soon as such qualities are proposed, it would be possible to write new books to fit that model, resulting in new divinely inspired works.

Sometimes, Protestants note that the biblical books occasionally quote each other as Scripture, either using the word *Scripture* itself or with equivalent formulas like "it is written," or "David, inspired by the Holy Spirit, said . . ." Does this mean the scriptures attest to themselves?

It does show one book can attest to *another* book, but this won't let you determine the canon as a whole. For that, you'd need every book of the Bible to be referred to as Scripture in another book, and that doesn't happen. Many books in the Protestant Bible aren't quoted as Scripture (or at all) by other books.

You specifically couldn't prove the New Testament canon. There are two only times a New Testament book refers to another as Scripture. The first is in 1 Timothy, where Paul quotes a passage that is *apparently* from Luke as Scripture (1 Tim. 5:18; cf. Luke 10:7), but you'd have to *first* know that 1 Timothy is Scripture for it to validate Luke. The second case is when Peter refers to Paul's letters as Scripture (2 Pet. 3:16), but here you'd not only have to know that 2 Peter is Scripture, you'd also have to know the list of Paul's letters, for Peter doesn't name them. Even if you knew these things, that would leave you with a canon consisting of Luke and Paul's letters (ironically, the canon proposed by the heretic Marcion).

But fundamentally, you'd need to show—apart from such quotations—that at least one book was Scripture. It doesn't prove anything if a non-scriptural book refers to another book as Scripture. Neither does a loop of mutual quotations. You'd need to prove the inspiration of at least one book by something outside of Scripture, which means you're not relying on Scripture alone.

Some have argued that historical evidence shows that the books of the New Testament are accurate. This is true, but historical accuracy isn't divine inspiration. Lots of books are historically accurate, but that doesn't make them Scripture. Also, this argument appeals to historical evidence, meaning the books of the Bible aren't self-attesting.

Others have proposed that the Holy Spirit attests to the heart of each believer that the books of the Bible are inspired. There are multiple problems with this argument:

- It departs from the principle of *sola scriptura* because one isn't appealing to the books of Scripture themselves but to a private revelation, whether it takes the form of a feeling, a voice, or something else.

- It is hard to square with the teachings of most Protestant churches, which hold that the age of such revelations ceased with the writing of the New Testament.

- No verses in the New Testament promise God will give believers such revelations, but we would need to prove this by Scripture alone to avoid violating *sola scriptura*.

- This principle isn't used in practice, for the typical Protestant doesn't read a book—in the Bible or outside it—and then ask God for a revelation about whether it is Scripture.

- Protestants actively discourage people from doing this when Mormons invite people to pray about whether the *Book of Mormon* is "another testament of Jesus Christ." They rightly recognize that God hasn't promised such private revelations, and it's dangerous in the extreme to decide what counts as Scripture by subjective feelings.

The truth is that when Protestants decide which books they recognize as Scripture, it's on the basis of tradition. At some point in their lives, someone hands them a Bible, and they accept the books it contains because they are found in that Bible. This is literally an act of *traditio*—a handing-over of the books of Scripture. It doesn't matter whether someone hands them the Bible in a church, a bookstore, or as a gift in a family setting. They still accept the books they do because they were handed on to them.

The question is whether this process of tradition was protected by God from error and what guarantees that to be the case, urgent matters for anyone wanting to employ *sola scriptura*. As an act of faith, a Protestant might conclude the Holy Spirit infallibly guided the Church into recognizing the books of the New Testament. Yet, that is a process that took centuries and involved popes and councils—the Magisterium. But if God infallibly guided the Magisterium in recognizing the books of the New Testament, consistency would demand that we see him as doing the same for the books of the Old Testament.

Protestants need to take the Catholic canon of Scripture seriously. The vast majority of Christians have always accepted the deuterocanonical books of the Old Testament. And the same chain of popes and councils that established the New Testament canon also endorsed them. Protestants themselves accept the canon they do on the basis of tradition, and the Protestant canon can't be supported using *sola scriptura*.

Ultimately, one must trust that God guided the Church on this, for it was the Catholic Church that gave the world the Bible.

THE BIBLE IS A CATHOLIC BOOK

Many groups seek to claim the Bible for themselves, but as we've seen, the Bible is a Catholic book!

Jesus Christ founded the Catholic Church, telling St. Peter, "You are Peter, and on this rock I will build my Church, and the powers of death shall not prevail against it" (Matt. 16:18). His Church has existed from that day until now. Jesus promised that he would be with his Church until the end of time (Matt. 28:20), and he promised that the Holy Spirit would lead the disciples "into all the truth" (John 16:12).

Jesus appointed the apostles to be authoritative teachers in his Church. They were the first generation of the Church's teaching authority, or Magisterium, and they began spreading the message of Jesus far and wide. They handed the Old Testament scriptures on to the Church, using both the Hebrew originals and the Greek Septuagint. They supplemented these by their oral preaching—the apostolic Tradition that was authoritative in the Church years before any New Testament scriptures were penned. They and their associates then began, under divine inspiration, to reduce some of the apostolic Tradition into writing, creating the New Testament.

Christians in the Apostolic Age understood that the word of God is contained both in Scripture and Tradition, which were to be understood in light of the teaching of the Magisterium. When the apostles passed from the scene, they handed over the government of the Church to men they appointed, the bishops, who became the next generation of the Church's Magisterium. At this time, the Catholic Church acquired its name. It was the universal (Greek, *katholikē*) Church, as distinguished from local sects.

Down through history, Christians followed the same principle used in the Apostolic Age, relying on Scripture, Tradition, and the Magisterium. This was true in the age of the Church Fathers in the Middle Ages and the modern era.

As the Catholic faith spread, it produced a rich literature. The Church Fathers wrote many works exploring the wonders of God's word, and Catholic missionaries began translating the scriptures into the languages of the lands they evangelized. One major translation was Jerome's Latin Vulgate, which became the most popular Bible in the West for centuries, and which is admired even by non-Catholic scholars. As new lands were evangelized, and as new languages like French, Spanish, German, and English developed, Catholics made translations into these languages as well.

Under the guidance of the Holy Spirit, the Catholic Church discerned which books belonged in the Bible, and in 382, Pope Damasus I established the canon of Scripture. This was reaffirmed by various local councils and popes and by the ecumenical Council of Florence in 1442. When the Protestant Reformation began, the Reformers attempted to decanonize certain books as Scripture, but the Council of Trent infallibly reaffirmed the canon in 1546.

Because the Reformers advocated ideas contradicting Tradition and the Magisterium, they rejected their authority and abandoned the principles Christians had used since the Apostolic Age, leaving them free to interpret Scripture however they desired. They advocated the novel principle that doctrine should be established *sola scriptura* or "by Scripture alone."

But *sola scriptura* is plagued with problems. If every doctrine must be proved by Scripture alone, then *sola scriptura* must be proved this way, and it can't be. Nobody dreamed of using this principle in the Apostolic Age when the apostles were authoritatively preaching the Christian message in the form of oral Tradition. Instead, the apostles ordered their followers to hold fast to both written and unwritten traditions (2 Thess. 2:15) and commended them for doing so (1 Cor. 11:2). There are no passages saying that this was to change after the apostles' time. As a doctrine, *sola scriptura* is self-refuting. It fails its own test.

Some anti-Catholics have made the ludicrous claim that the Catholic Church "hates" the Bible, but the Church has always considered the Bible sacred. That's why it spread copies of it in every land and language.

It's also why we have the Bible to begin with. It was a labor of love for Catholics to make copies of it in the days when books were fantastically expensive and had to be copied by hand. The monks treasured the Bible so much they even made beautiful, illuminated copies—literally covering its pages with gold—to give glory to God for the gift of his word. If they had not performed this labor, the original manuscripts would have perished and we would have no copies of the Bible today. We owe them an enormous debt for preserving the scriptures, patiently and carefully copying them, and making them available throughout the world.

Protestants must be frank with themselves: They have the Bible only because of the Catholic Church. They accept the books of the Bible that they do on the basis of tradition, and God guided the Church to recognizing the canon it did by sorting the true books of Scripture from false ones. They wouldn't have the Bible if it were not for the Catholic Church.

Catholics have every reason to take pride in the Bible. It's a precious gift that God used the Catholic Church to give to the world.

So where should you go from here? How can you learn more about this marvelous gift?

Everyone should read the Bible and study its teachings. We are fortunate to live in an age when many fine translations are available—and they are amazingly inexpensive compared with every previous age! Only a lack of gratitude to God would keep someone from plunging into God's written word and drinking from this rich fountain.

If you prefer modern translations, there are many. The *Revised Standard Version: Catholic Edition* is an excellent literal translation. The U.S. Catholic bishops publish the *New American Bible*, which is a modern, dynamic translation. And if you like reading the Bible in an older, elevated style, the Douay-Rheims is still in print.

Many Bibles come with extensive prefaces and study notes, and there are countless Scripture-study tools available, including Bible dictionaries, commentaries, and study guides. There is even Bible software that uses the power of information-processing technology to unearth even more insights from God's word.

To help ensure you understand Scripture's message correctly, you should do what people have since the days of the apostles: read it in light of the apostolic Tradition and the Magisterium Christ gave his Church. In addition to studying Scripture, you should read the Church Fathers and the documents of the Church. The *Catechism of the Catholic Church* is an excellent starting point. To learn what the Church teaches about Scripture itself, you can read *Dei Verbum* (*The Word of God*), Vatican II's constitution on divine revelation, and Pope Benedict

XVI's apostolic exhortation *Verbum Domini* (*The Word of the Lord*).

However you study Scripture, be sure to take it to heart. Whether you are using a traditional, prayerful study technique like *lectio divina* or parsing Greek verbs with modern Bible software, open yourself to the scriptures and let them transform your life.

It's time to get started!

APPENDIX I

Bible Timeline

Scholars debate the exact chronology of biblical events. The dates below are based on my own calculations. For more information, I recommend Jack Finegan's book, *Handbook of Biblical Chronology*, rev. ed.[62] and Andrew E. Steinmann's book, *From Abraham to Paul*.[63]

NOTE: "ca." is short for *circa* (Latin, "around").

The Old Testament Period

2000s B.C.	Life of Abraham (early dating)
1800s B.C.	Life of Abraham (late dating)
1400s B.C.	Exodus from Egypt (early dating)
1200s B.C.	Exodus from Egypt (late dating)
1048 B.C.	Reign of King Saul begins
1009 B.C.	Reign of King David begins
971 B.C.	Reign of King Solomon begins
932 B.C.	Kingdoms of Israel and Judah separate
723 B.C.	Israel falls to Assyrians
586 B.C.	Jerusalem falls to Babylonians (temple destroyed; Exile begins)
515 B.C.	Rebuilt temple dedicated
331 B.C.	Palestine conquered by Alexander the Great
169 B.C.	Antiochus IV desecrates the temple (Maccabees rebel)
63 B.C.	Romans take control of Judaea (Maccabean rule ended)
36 B.C.	Herod the Great becomes king in Jerusalem

The New Testament Period

3/2 B.C.	Jesus born
1 B.C.	Herod the Great dies
A.D. 10	Jesus found in the temple (Luke 2)
14	Augustus dies; Tiberius becomes emperor

26	Pontius Pilate becomes governor of Judaea
29	The ministries of John the Baptist and Jesus begin
33	The Crucifixion (April 3)
36	Pontius Pilate recalled to Rome; martyrdom of Stephen (Acts 7); conversion of Paul (Acts 9)
37	Tiberius dies; Caligula becomes emperor
ca. 40	Conversion of the household of Cornelius (Acts 10)
41	Caligula assassinated; Claudius becomes emperor
43	James, son of Zebedee, martyred at Jerusalem (Acts 12:1–2)
43–49	Paul's First Missionary Journey (Acts 13–14)
ca. 48	The letter of James written
49	Council of Jerusalem (Acts 15)
49–51	Paul's Second Missionary Journey (Acts 15:40–18:22)
ca. 50	1 Thessalonians, 2 Thessalonians, Galatians written
51–55	Paul's Third Missionary Journey (Acts 18:23–21:17)
ca. 53	1 Corinthians written
54	Claudius poisoned; Nero becomes emperor
ca 54–55	2 Corinthians, Romans written
55	Paul arrested in Jerusalem (Acts 21:26–36)
ca 55	Gospel of Mark written
57	Paul sent to Rome for trial before Nero (Acts 27:1)
58	Paul arrives in Rome (Acts 28:11–16)
59	Gospel of Luke written
ca. 58–60	Ephesians, Philippians, Colossians, Philemon written
60	Book of Acts written
62	James the Just martyred at Jerusalem
ca. 62–63	1 Peter written
ca. 63	Gospel of Matthew written
ca. 64–65	2 Peter and Jude written
ca. 65	Gospels of John written; also 1 Timothy, Titus, and 1–3 John
65–66	Peter martyred at Rome
66	Great Jewish Revolt Begins

ca 66	2 Timothy written
67	Paul martyred at Rome
68	Nero forced to commit suicide; Galba becomes emperor
ca. 68	Hebrews and Revelation written
69	The chaotic "Year of Four Emperors": Galba, Otho, Vitellius, and Vespasian each serve as emperor
70	*1 Clement* written; Roman forces take Jerusalem and destroy the temple
73	Last Jewish holdouts at Masada commit suicide; Great Jewish Revolt ends

Later History of the Bible

382	Pope Damasus I holds the Council of Rome, which establishes the canon of Scripture
383	St. Jerome begins translating the Latin Vulgate
393	Council of Hippo reaffirms the canon
397	Council of Carthage reaffirms the canon
405	Pope Innocent I reaffirms the canon
419	Another Council of Carthage reaffirms the canon
1442	The Council of Florence reaffirms the canon
ca. 1439	Johannes Gutenberg develops the printing press
ca. 1454	The Gutenberg Bible printed
1517	Martin Luther begins the Protestant Reformation
1546	The Council of Trent infallibly reaffirms the traditional canon of Scripture
1582	Catholic Rheims New Testament published
1609–10	Catholic Douay Old Testament published
1611	Protestant King James Version published
1965	Vatican II issues *Dei Verbum*, the Dogmatic Constitution on Divine Revelation
1978	John Paul II issues the *Nova Vulgata*, an updated edition of Jerome's Latin Vulgate

APPENDIX II

Glossary

antilegomena: (Greek, *anti-* "against" + *legô* "speak") Books of the New Testament that were spoken against by some—i.e., Hebrews, James, 2 Peter, 2–3 John, Jude, and Revelation (Eusebius, *Church History* 3:3, 24, 25).

apocrypha: (Greek, *apokruphos*, "hidden") In Protestant circles, this term refers to the books of the Old Testament that Catholics refer to as deuterocanonical (e.g., 2 Maccabees). In Catholic circles, it refers to non-canonical books associated with the Old Testament (e.g., *Jubilees*) or the New Testament (e.g., *Protoevangelium of James*).

canon: (Greek, *kanôn*, "rod, rule") The set or list of divinely inspired books that count as Scripture.

catholic epistles: Letters of the New Testament addressed primarily to a general audience rather than a specific church. In practice, the non-Pauline letters (James, 1–2 Peter, 1–3 John, and Jude).

codex: A book with the pages attached to a spine—i.e., the modern form of a book read by flipping the pages (cf., "Scroll").

council: A gathering of bishops. Councils may be local, in which case they have authority in a particular territory, or ecumenical, in which case their authority is worldwide.

deuterocanonical: (Greek, *deuteros*, "second" + canon) Books that achieved recognition as canonical second. The Catholic Church recognizes 1–2 Maccabees, Tobit, Judith, Baruch,

Sirach, Wisdom, and parts of Daniel and Esther as deutero-canonical (cf., "Protocanonical").

epistle: (Greek, *epistolê*) Another term for a letter.

epitome: (Greek, *epitomê*, "cutting") An abridgment of a longer work.

inspiration: The gift of the Holy Spirit that assisted a human author to write a biblical book so that it has God as its author and teaches faithfully, without error, the saving truth that God has willed to be consigned to us.

"Law, the": Another term for the Pentateuch ("the Law of Moses").

Magisterium: (Latin, *magister*, "teacher") The teaching authority Christ gave his Church; the men who exercise this authority (the bishops in union with the pope).

papyrus: Writing material made from the Egyptian papyrus reed.

parchment: Writing material made from animal skin.

pastoral epistles: Letters St. Paul wrote to pastors (1–2 Timothy, Titus).

Pentateuch: (Greek, *pentateuchos*, "five-volume work") The first five books of the Bible (Genesis, Exodus, Leviticus, Numbers, and Deuteronomy).

prison epistles: Letters St. Paul wrote in prison (Ephesians, Philippians, Colossians, 2 Timothy, Philemon).

protocanonical: (Greek, *prôtos*, "first" + canon) Books which achieved recognition as canonical first (cf., "Deuterocanonical")—i.e., the books included in the modern Hebrew Bible and the Protestant Old Testament.

scribe: A person trained to write.

Scripture: (Latin, *scriptura*, "writing") A book written under divine inspiration; the set of books written under inspiration.

scroll: A book with the pages attached side-by-side and read by rolling and unrolling rather than flipping the pages (cf., "Codex").

testament: A covenant, a sacred agreement. The books of the Bible are either those associated with the covenants God made with the Jewish people (the Old Testament) or the New Covenant he made through Christ (the New Testament).

Torah: (Hebrew, "instruction") Another term for the Pentateuch.

tradition: (Latin, *traditio,* "handing down") That which is handed down from one person or generation to another. Sacred Tradition refers to those things handed down from Christ and the apostles. When lower cased, *tradition* may refer to nonauthoritative ideas or practices.

Wisdom Literature: Books of the Old Testament that convey wisdom in various forms (Job, Psalms, Proverbs, Ecclesiastes, Song of Solomon, Wisdom, and Sirach)

ENDNOTES

1   See Gary Rendsburg, *The Redaction of Genesis* (1986, repr. University Park: Pennsylvania State University Press, 2017); and Isaac Kikawada and Arthur Quinn, *Before Abraham Was: The Unity of Genesis 1–11* (1985, repr. Eugene, OR: Wipf and Stock, 2017).

2   *General Audience*, May 8, 1985.

3   Ibid.

4   *Antiquities* 17:2:4.

5   Ibid., 18:1:5.

6   Hippolytus, *Philosophumena* 9:29; Origen, *Against Celsus* 1:49; Commentary on Matthew 17:35–36; Jerome, Commentary on Matthew 3:22:31–32.

7   For citations from rabbinic literature concerning these books, see Lee M. McDonald, *The Formation of the Biblical Canon* (New York: Bloomsbury T&T Clark, 2017), 1:396–398.

8   Josephus, *The Jewish War* 1:2:8.

9   *Who Is the Heir of Divine Things* 52.

10 *On the Cherubim* 9.

11 *On the Migration of Abraham* 7.

12 Josephus, *Jewish War* 6:5:3.

13 *b. Baba Bathra* 4a.

14 See Gleason L. Archer and G.C. Chirichingo, *Old Testament Quotations in the New Testament: A Complete Survey* (Chicago: Moody Press, 1983) for an index of Jesus' quotations of the Old Testament in the Gospels.

15 See Archer and Chirichingo, *Old Testament Quotations.*

16 Archer and Chirichingo classify 340 quotations as being based, with variations, on the Septuagint (their categories A, B, and D) compared to 33 based on the Hebrew Masoretic text (their category C); see xxv–xxxii.

17 James D. G. Dunn, *Word Biblical Commentary, Vol. 38A: Romans 1–8* (Dallas: Word Books, 1988), 72; biblical citations adapted for clarity.

18 *Antiquities* 17:2:4.

19 For an excellent discussion of letters in the ancient world, see E. Randolph Richards, *Paul and First-Century Letter Writing: Secretaries, Composition, and Collection* (Downers Grove, IL: InterVarsity Press, 2004).

20 Richards, *Paul and First-Century Letter Writing*, 163.

21 Ibid., 169.

22 For a full discussion of *hypomnêmata* and *comentarii*, see Matthew D.C. Larsen, *Gospels Before the Book* (Oxford, England: Oxford University Press, 2018).

23 See Jimmy Akin, "The Cost of the Gospels and the Synoptic Problem," JimmyAkin. com, January 30, 2016, http://jimmyakin.com/2016/01/the-cost-of-the-gospels-and-the-synoptic-problem.html.

24 See Richard Bauckham, ed., *The Gospels for All Christians: Rethinking the Gospel Audiences* (Grand Rapids, MI: Eerdmans, 1997).

25 See Martin Hengel, *Studies in the Gospel of Mark* (London: SCM Press, 1985), chap. 3.

26 See Richard Bauckham, *Jesus and the Eyewitnesses*, 2nd ed. (Grand Rapids, MI: Eerdmans, 2017), chaps. 14–17; and Benedict XVI, *Jesus of Nazareth*, Vol. 1 (New

York: Doubleday, 2007), chap. 8.

27　See Matthew D.C. Larsen, *Gospels Before the Book* (Oxford, England: Oxford University Press, 2018).

28　Eusebius, *Church History* 3:15.

29　See Jimmy Akin, "Did John Use Mark as a Template?," JimmyAkin.com, November 15, 2014, https://jimmyakin.com/2014/11/did-john-use-mark-as-a-template.html.

30　Josephus, *Jewish War* 7:6:6; Suetonius, *The Twelve Caesars*, "Domitian" 12:2.

31　*Against Heresies* 3:1.

32　*Church History* 2:22:1–2.

33　See Jack Finegan, *Handbook of Biblical Chronology*, 2nd ed. (Peabody, MA: Hendrickson Publishers, 1998); and Andrew Steinmann, *From Abraham to Paul* (St. Louis, MO: Concordia Publishing, 2011).

34　See Eusebius, *Ecclesiastical History* 2:22:2.

35　Jerome, *Lives of Illustrious Men* 5.

36　Tacitus, *Annals* 15:44.

37　*1 Clement* 5.

38　Jerome, *Lives of Illustrious Men* 59.

39　*On Modesty* 20.

40　Eusebius, *Church History* 6:25:14.

41　Josephus, *Antiquities of the Jews*, 20:9:1.

42　Eusebius, *Church History* 3:39:6.

43　See David Trobisch, *Paul's Letter Collection* (Bolivar, MO: Quiet Waters, 2001), for an extensive discussion of this topic.

44　*1 Clement* 5.

45　Irenaeus, *Against Heresies* 1:26:3.

46　Hippolytus, *Refutation of All Heresies* 7:24.

47　Clement of Alexandria, *Stromateis* 2:20, 3:4.

48　Letter to the Smyrneans, 8:1–2.

49　*First Apology* 67.

50　*Church History* 3:25:1–6 with 3:3:5–6.

51　*Enchiridion Symbolorum* 179–180.

52　Ibid., 213.

53　These latter councils did not explicitly mention Lamentations and Baruch, but these were commonly reckoned as part of Jeremiah.

54　*Against Rufinus* 2:33.

55　Bruce M. Metzger, *The Bible in Translation: Ancient and English Versions* (Grand Rapids, MI: Baker Academic, 2001), 29–30.

56　Letter 71.

57　Metzger, *The Bible in Translation*, 35.

58　Samuel Jackson, ed., *The New Schaff-Herzog Encyclopedia of Religious Knowledge* (New York: Funk and Wagnalls, 1908), 2:144.

59　Ibid., 56.

60　*Enchiridion Symbolorum* 1501–1504.

61　Ibid., 1335.

62　Peabody, MA: Hendrickson Publishers, 1998.

63　St. Louis, MO: Concordia Publishing, 2011.

About the Author

Jimmy Akin is an internationally known author and speaker. As the senior apologist at Catholic Answers, he has more than twenty-five years of experience defending and explaining the Faith.

Jimmy is a convert to the Faith and has an extensive background in the Bible, theology, the Church Fathers, philosophy, canon law, and liturgy. Jimmy is a weekly guest on the national radio program Catholic Answers Live, a regular contributor to *Catholic Answers Magazine*, and a popular blogger and podcaster. His books include *The Fathers Know Best* and *A Daily Defense*. His personal website is JimmyAkin.com.

Join Us in the Vineyard!

Catholic Answers is in the business of saving souls.

We need your help to do that, because we're an independent, nonprofit organization. We don't ask for or receive financial support from any diocese.

Instead, Catholic Answers is supported by the generosity of individual Catholics who understand the value of the work we do explaining and defending the Faith.

Your donations make our soul-saving work possible.

Won't you join us? For your convenience, there are several ways to make your tax-deductible donation.

You can:

Visit give.catholic.com/donate
Call 888-291-8000
Mail Send checks to:

Catholic Answers
2020 Gillespie Way
El Cajon, CA 92020

Catholic Answers is a 501(c)3 nonprofit organization.

What Is Catholic Answers?

Catholic Answers is a media ministry that serves Christ by explaining and defending the Catholic faith:

- We help Catholics grow in their faith
- We bring former Catholics home
- We lead non-Catholics into the fullness of the truth

There are many ways we help people:

 Catholic Answers Live is America's most popular Catholic radio program

 Catholic Answers Press publishes faith-building books, booklets, magazines, and audio resources

 Catholic Answers Studios creates television programs, DVDs, and online videos

 Our website, Catholic.com hosts hundreds of thousands of online resources, free to use

 Catholic Answers Events conducts seminars, conferences, and pilgrimages

Catholic Answers is an independent, nonprofit organization supported by your donations.

Visit us online and learn how we can help you.

Your journey starts at:
catholic.com